Auks, Rocks and the Odd Dinosaur

Auks, Rocks and

Inside Stories from the

Thomas Y. Crowell
New York

Peggy Thomson

the Odd Dinosaur

Smithsonian's Museum of Natural History

Photo credits: Chip Clark, jacket bottom left, 13, 16 left, 22 top, 26, 30, 34, 38 top and bottom, 41, 42 left and right, 51 left, 54, 58, 66, 69, 70, 74, 76, 78, 80, 82, 86, 88, 93, 94, 101, 102 top, 104 bottom, 106, 108, 110 inset, 115; Paul Conklin, 110; Naval Surface Weapons Center, 102 bottom; Dane Penland, jacket top, 44; Charles Phillips, 2, 8 top and bottom; Smithsonian Institution, jacket bottom right, 10 and inset, 22 bottom, 32 bottom, 36, 51 right, 56, 62, 65, 85, 98, 104 top; Smithsonian Institution Anthropological Archive, 16 right, 18; Smithsonian Institution Archives, 28; Smithsonian Institution Archives Photograph Collection, 5, 26 inset, 29; Smithsonian Institution National Portrait Gallery, 32 top.

The story of the Plains Indian woman and her navel-cord bag which appears on page 96 is reprinted from Annals of the New York Academy of Sciences with the generous permission of the author, John C. Ewers, and of the New York Academy of Sciences.

Library of Congress Cataloging in Publication Data
Thomson, Peggy,
  Auks, rocks and the odd dinosaur.

  Summary; Reveals the inner workings of the National Museum of Natural History through historical anecdotes and descriptions of how exhibits are researched, prepared, and maintained.
  1. National Museum of Natural History—Juvenile literature. [1. National Museum of Natural History. 2. Museums] I. National Museum of Natural History. II. Title.
  QH70.U62W278 1985   508'.074'0153   85-47744
  ISBN 0-690-04491-7
  ISBN 0-690-04492-5 (lib. bdg.)

Designed by Constance Fogler
1 2 3 4 5 6 7 8 9 10
First Edition

For

JOHN SEABURY T.,

whose natural history museum is
the Potomac River

ACKNOWLEDGMENTS

My special thanks go to James Mello, Stanwyn Shetler, Harold Banks for reading chapters along the way and to the museum's docents—Betsy Leedy, Joan Madden, Laura McKie, Rebecca Mead, Magda Schremp—for educating, for sharing their sense of fun, for spotting blunders; to Ray Rye, whose talents include talking paleontology to a beginner; to auks men Storrs Olson, Phil Angle; to archivists Bill Deiss, Paula Fleming, Pam Henson; to Eskimo archaeologists Henry Collins, William Fitzhugh; to patcher of giraffes Frank Greenwell, mineralogist Dan Appleman, conservator Caroline Rose; to the teller of gem tales Mary Winters, house-mouse man Joe Marshall, tarantulas' mom Kay Weisberg; to anthropologist Jennifer Kelley for introducing me to the matter of the soap man's underwear; and to guards William Wells and Marvin Dorsey, who let me tag along on a night's rounds with dog Max.

Special thanks, too, to Chip Clark, who took most of the photographs, and to photographer Paul Conklin, who provided crucial extras; to the knowledgeable Unflappables, Tom Harney (at the museum), Jan Solow (at Harper & Row); and to the Monday Group of the Children's Book Guild who responded to each *Auks, Rocks* chapter with their complaints and good cheer—Larry Callen, Helen Jacob, Gloria Kamen, Marguerite Murray, Gene Namovicz, Phyllis Naylor.

Contents

Auks, Rocks and
the Odd Dinosaur

African bush elephant in rotunda greets six million visitors a year. Hide is real, but tusks are lightweight fiberglass copies.

Introduction

THE great auk is scruffy of feather. The bull mummy from Egypt has something not quite right about its interior. So does the pickled rift worm. The Hope diamond has a cops-and-robbers past. It's not perfect either. And the tail of the flesh-eating dinosaur *Antrodemus* does not match the body, for good reason.

Bird, bull, worm, gem, dinosaur—they are treasures of the National Museum of Natural History. The diamond is worth a fortune, but then so are the others, though they are rag and skin and bone. While some are very plain to look at, they become special as their inside stories are known.

You may meet them all face to face in Washington, DC, where Natural History, as part of the Smithsonian Institution, stands next door to American History and catty-cornered to Air and Space. Or you may meet them, along with other special objects, in the pages of this book.

In the museum you'll find the great auk and the rest scattered through the exhibit halls upstairs and down. Most are behind glass. Some, like the Indian tiger, stand free where they need vacuum cleaning and an eyeballs wash.

A few, like the buffalo hair balls, are on view where they can be handled. "Stumpers" such as these are intended to puzzle, which is why they appear with question marks and invitations to touch.

At least one stumper also stumped the scientists, who thought a lumpy rock was a fossilized dinosaur dropping. Then they learned it was not.

If you seek out each of these objects on foot, you will meet guards and guard dogs on patrol, and you will walk more than two miles.

Guards, ever on the lookout, say they see three types of visitors. They see Commuters, who rush in one door and out another, using the museum for a shortcut; Cruisers, who dip in and out of halls, drifting; and Very much Interested People, who head straight for Dinosaurs or the Insect Zoo or Gems. The VIPs, though they become sidetracked like anyone else, seem to have a plan, and some of them cover exhibits inch by inch.

The museum serves everyone. But mostly it serves science. It does so by collecting and by scrutinizing all that it collects—birds, beasts, rocks, bugs, plants, fish and not only these, but the tools and clothes of primitive peoples, their vocabularies, their dreams and myths. The museum gathers them, studies them, saves them, shows them. For the history of the planet and its inhabitants is read from these bones and tools just as information is read from books.

One man—Spencer Fullerton Baird—began the museum's collecting. When he was hired in 1850 as the Smithsonian's assistant head (there wasn't then, or for many years to come, a separate natural history museum), he brought along his own natural history collection. It was the best in the country, containing birds of 500 species, mammals, reptiles, fishes in great numbers and fossil bones. It filled two railroad boxcars. Some of it Baird had gathered as a boy on country bird walks with an older brother. He'd gathered more as a youth, by this time walking alone, whistling tunes and reciting poetry to entertain himself. In the year he was 19, he'd covered 2,100

Space to store odd-shaped objects was a problem even in the 1890s.

miles, sometimes 40 or 50 in a day, and he wore out three sets of soles to his boots.

There wasn't then a formal training program in natural history, so Baird studied medicine for a year. Mostly he learned by observation and reading and teaching. (He taught his pupils outdoors, on field trips.) He also learned by corresponding with experienced naturalists. A letter he wrote about a flycatcher to bird painter James Audubon won him a lifetime tutor and friend, who replied that Baird had an "old head" on a boy's shoulders. When Baird later wanted a letter of "flaming recommendation" to get a museum job in Washington, Audubon was glad to write it.

Even heartily recommended, Baird did not get the job for four more years, not until he was 27. When he did (and brought along

5

his boxcars of skins and bones), he proved himself a demon worker. He made order out of the mountains of crates and bales and barrels inherited from the United States Exploring Expedition, and he said he was ready for more. At that time the U.S. Government was sending numbers of exploring parties to patrol borders and to survey, to plot railroad routes across the Rocky Mountains and to build wagon roads. Baird, seeing the great possibilities, trained many of the travelers—army doctors and soldiers—to collect for him along with their other duties. They carried collecting equipment in their packs. They pressed plants and skinned specimens by campfires, shipping things back when they could.

In addition, Baird sent out his own people, who enlisted still others—trappers and traders and missionaries, even lighthouse keepers, who provided him with whales. He had a whole network. One of his men said there was not a schoolboy with a talent for fishing or finding nests whom Baird didn't know and encourage.

Baird equipped his collectors from Washington. He sent them kegs of alcohol and ammunition, fish-collecting trunks, sieves, insect pins and advice: how to stitch extra pockets to jackets, how to pickle a skin and how to pack eggs in twists of paper, not in moss. "Try hard for salamanders," he urged in a letter, "some in water, some on land, under logs." He added, "I won't give much for a live ostrich, but will give a bottle of first rate Scuppernong wine . . . for his skeleton."

To all, without a typewriter, without a secretary, he wrote long, cheering, newsy letters. One young collector replied that Baird's letters made him "feel strong in the backbone." Baird also never forgot to describe his excitement on opening the packets from the field. He named new species after their faraway finders. And the finders named new species—some 40—for him, among them a

Baird's tapir, a Baird's octopus, a Baird's dolphin and a Baird's sandpiper. Audubon gave the name to a Baird's sparrow.

Some of the young collectors Baird put to work in Washington. They had a club called the Megatherium Club, which held oyster roasts and had special yells. They gathered at Baird's house, invited by Mrs. Baird, who won her husband's affection with the fine labels she wrote for his specimens. In snatches of time from other museum duties Baird wrote huge volumes on the birds, fishes, snakes and mammals of North America. When he wrote at home, he kept a small barrel of reptiles by his desk for his little daughter Lucy to play with.

In the Baird years the collections began their rapid growth—to 2 million things at the time of his death, to 68 million now. Collections grow as natural history collections have to grow. For one single animal does not tell the story of its species. Whether it's a rhinoceros or a shellfish the size of a speck of dust, examples are needed of male, female and young; from times past and present; from this locality, from that; collected in winter, in spring, in sickness, in health.

Collections also grow because scientists, who are everywhere, diving, digging, chipping, scanning, keep finding new and different things. Beyond the 26 million insects at hand, they net new and different insects in the canopies of trees. They scoop them from the dew in tire treads, pick them off snowfields and cactuses.

In similar ways vast numbers of new things are gathered up, not out of greediness, but from a need to fill in gaps and chinks. In Baird's day the rush was on to collect everything. Now there's still a rush, for species go extinct. But there's a lid on collecting. Restraint comes from the danger of depleting supplies in nature and from the awful problems of storage and care. Scientists admit they

Lineup of taxidermied animals in museum attic and drawers of eggs are part of vast study collections not seen by the public.

still *want* everything, but they are agonizingly selective about what they take.

The objects on exhibit are a tiny fraction of the collections. Even the visitors who look at everything and think they've seen the museum haven't really seen it. They've seen the *exhibits.* Some things are too fragile to go out on view, and some are needed for study.

Visitors don't see the scientists at work. That part of the museum is out of sight, where people are decoding the patterns in minerals and photographing ticks' tongues and where one person is recording frog jumps while another is testing the breaks in mastodon bones. Were the bones broken by the trampling of other animals or by ancient peoples, getting at marrow for food? It makes a difference for dating when human beings first came to North America.

Except for the coral reef, which has windows into its lab, the labs are closed to the public. So is the huge new $50-million "closet," a storage complex out beyond the city limits where totem poles and bamboos get just the temperature and humidity they need.

Visitors see a sample of the whole, just as the items in this book are a sampling of the exhibits. Meet these scraps and pieces close up—the great auk, precious rocks, *Antrodemus* and the rest. Learn their inside stories and some information and gossip you will not find on their labels.

The penguinlike great auk, now extinct, and its large five-inch egg were fancied by seafarers as food in the early 1800s.

Great Auk

MEET the great auk for a start—a big, bottle-shaped, stand-up seabird with stubby wings and a white splotch by each eye. Its skin and feathers are real. And that's rare, not just because great auks have been extinct for 140 years, but because they disappeared so fast that few skins were saved.

The museum bought this bird early, already mounted. It was collected in 1834, the same year that the last great auk in England died—of eating potatoes. In the early days the museum also owned a great auk leg bone and a large, spotted great auk egg, which is kept today under lock and key in a high-security cabinet. It is lucky to have such specimens, never mind that the feathers are scruffy or that spots on the egg are blurred from a long-ago scrubbing it never should have had. Only consider that even 100 years ago one great auk egg sold at auction for $1,200; and that recently a museum paid $12,000 for one of the 79 known great auk skins.

All the same, in the 1880s Frederic Lucas of the museum staff thought that one skin, one bone and one egg were a skimpy record of a remarkable species. The clowny-looking birds had been gone for 40 years. It made him sad: no naturalist had ever met one alive or seen it walk its wobbly walk or fly, as it did, underwater, swimming. (Great auks, like penguins, were flightless.) Lucas believed time was running out for learning the birds' secrets.

When Lucas dug his great auks, Leonhard Stejneger from the museum was collecting bones of the Steller sea cow in the North Pacific. He got the only complete skeleton to be seen anywhere.

The sea cows, which looked like a cross between whales and seals, had been discovered off the Commander Islands in 1741 by the stranded crew of the Bering Expedition. And naturalist Georg Steller, a member of the party, had described them—telling how harmless they were, browsing through beds of kelp like sheep grazing, how fearless of men and how affectionate to one another. When animals were injured, the others would try, often successfully, to knock harpoons from their bodies. Meat from the butchered sea cows nourished the party that winter. It was not only delicious, with a taste of almond to the fat, but it cured sailors of the scurvy.

In 1887 on the schooner *Grampus* he sailed into the North Atlantic on a collecting trip. He carried with him his camping gear and his clam hoes, and off the coast of Newfoundland he rowed himself ashore at rocky, uninhabited Funk Island to do his digging.

Lucas knew from his reading that each spring the birds had flocked to this tiny half-mile island (and to a very few others like it) for breeding; that they had covered every patch of turf with their big bodies, standing as close to one another as stones on a cobbled pavement.

There was no mystery, either, to how the birds had been wiped out. Flightless and predictable, coming year in, year out to Funk, they made easy targets. And they were enormously useful.

Eskimos and Indians hunted them. So did explorers and fisher-

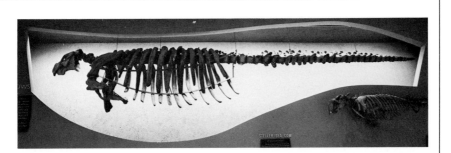

Word spread of the useful and docile beasts. Their rumpled skin, tough and elastic, served well as a covering for wooden boats and as shoe leather. Hunters, seeking the furs of otters and foxes, provisioned themselves with the meat. Sometimes instead of making a kill they simply sliced off chunks from the animals, who protested only with thrashings of their tails. Within 27 years of their discovery, the sea cows were extinct.

men from Europe. They caught them for food, for bait, for fuel. (Wood was scarce and the fat bodies burned like bundles of oily rags.) In the sixteenth century sailors drove the birds like sheep up gangplanks from shore to ship and used them to provision long voyages. By the early nineteenth century whole crews were on the island, killing birds for oil and for feathers to make hats. They boiled birds by the hundreds of thousands and left the carcasses.

Lucas saw the evidence. Bones stuck out everywhere, and the turf was sprinkled with eggshells. Slabs of granite lying all about looked to him like the birds' tombstones. He had hoped to find a great auk mummy, as sometimes happens, or even perfect skeletons. Instead he found only jumbles of bones. While puffins watched, he dug with his hoes and his fingers. He filled two barrels with the best of the bones. He filled one crate with bones just as he found them—good bones and not so good, complete with the peaty soil that surrounded them.

On his return to Washington he recorded his findings and made up skeletons from the pieces. Today his skeletons and what was left over of his best great auk bones fill large cabinets in the Birds division, and until five years ago, Lucas's crate of bones and dirt sat, still packed, in the basement.

Then a curator in the Birds division decided it was time to tidy up. Picking out the auk bones and sorting them was easy. The dirt was another matter. Because it wasn't trash dirt but historic dirt that might yield secrets, it had to be washed through screens and all the bits of it studied under a microscope.

What turned up, separated out from the peat, was a little pile of bony stuff that fits in a matchbox. It includes seven great auk ear bones and scales and pinhead-sized vertebrae from six kinds of fish.

The tidying was a bore—not like the setting sail and rowing ashore and digging that Lucas did. It took weeks of work. There was also no surprise about the findings. But the curator can now say which six species of fish once swam in the shallows around Funk Island. He cannot say for certain that the fish bones in the dirt came from the birds' stomachs. He thinks they did, but a passing seagull, taken sick, could have spat them. Anyway the list of What Some Great Auks (probably) Ate is now on record. And it was possible, after saving it for 90 years, to throw the dirt in the trash.

Kachina Doll

THE kachina doll hangs on the wall of a pueblo apartment where Indian women are grinding corn. It's a male doll, carved from the root of a cottonwood tree, with bright stripy clothing painted on, garters at the knees and a mask. There's a necklace of acorn shells around the neck and soft fluff from an eagle's breast on the headdress.

Kachinas were spirit beings who carried messages, mostly prayer messages asking for rain, for their kin in the "daylight" world. During ceremonies, men from the pueblos dressed as the kachinas and danced long, fantastic dances, their eyes a-glitter behind the slits in their masks.

When they paused to rest, other men, wearing warty masks smeared with pink mud, entertained the crowds. The mudheads clowned and sang and told rude jokes, and they carried little presents. Peering, pouncing and falling back again, they'd pretend it was hard to find the children in the crowd. Then they'd hold out a doll such as this one, coming closer and closer, until a mother would urge her child to take it.

The doll was not an idol, but not exactly a toy either. The gift of it was an initiation into life's mystery, a reminder that spirits with rain on their breath were ever present and powerful.

This doll was collected 100 years ago by Frank Cushing, who

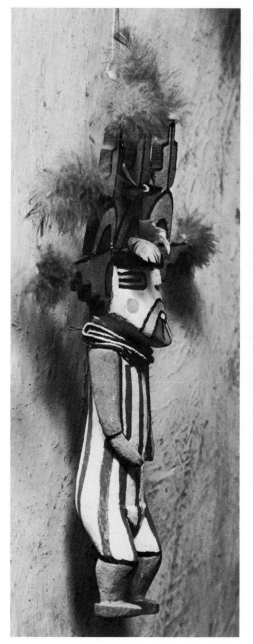

Frank Cushing (above) posed in the museum as a mudhead like those who gave kachina dolls (left) to children during Zuni ceremonies.

was sent at the age of 22 to learn about the Indians of the Southwest desert. The museum intended him to stay for three months. He stayed instead for five years, settling in and adopting the ways of the Zunis. He was a tall, bony figure, pasty white, who was half laughed at, half admired for what he did.

Early on, he let it be known he'd come to look and to learn. Then for a still closer look, he moved into the home of the head chief. Uninvited, he took along his books and papers and set up his hammock in a corner, saying he wished to learn the Indians' inner life.

The chief said "Tuh!" which was a kind of oath, and asked why. After all, he said, the Zunis had one religion and Cushing's people had another, and that was that. But Cushing said there were fools among his people back East who thought the Indians had *no* religion, and he wished to show them wrong.

The chief replied that there were fools among the Indians, too, who might harm a white person. But he let the young man stay. Weeks later when he saw Cushing looking sad and lonely one day, he said to him, "Little brother . . . if . . . you will only make up your mind to be a Zuni . . . you shall have fathers and mothers, brothers and sisters" here with us. To do so Cushing would have to give up his "rabbit net," which is what the chief called his hammock, for if some night Cushing fell out of it, the Government might say the Indians had killed him. He must sleep on the ground like a man and give up his pig grease (bacon) and eat Zuni mutton and corn cakes. He would have to get rid of his hat with the mouse-head shape and his "squeaking foot packs" and wear a proper headband and moccasins. For, said the chief, "I want to make a Zuni of you." Cushing agreed to the terms, which is just as well. The chief had thrown out his clothes.

Frank Cushing, 1880s, in the outfit he said Zunis urged him to wear.

And so Cushing was more or less accepted, though the chief's wife sometimes dropped his meat on the ground and stepped on it before serving him. And more than once Indians complained about his sketching and his note taking, especially at ceremonies.

When Cushing heard the toomtoom and clang of drums and rattles and bells, he'd snatch his book bag from the antlers where it hung, ready for him to run and sketch a dance. But his Indian companion would say, "Be dignified, put down the paper fold and mind your own matters." When he went anyway, certain Indians threatened to cut his papers into pieces. They also threatened to throw him over a cliff, but Cushing held his ground and brandished his knife. Other Indians stood up for him, and he won his right to continue scribbling.

He lived the Zuni life, learning from an old blind man how he spun his wool, from the women how they singed their bangs, and from the grandmothers how they baked dumplings. He learned how meat was made into jerky, how tools and looms were made, and how clay was coiled for pots and the pots smothered in manure to fire them to a black finish. At festival times he'd note down all the preparations: how men stitched new clothing for themselves and their wives, how women wove new blankets and baskets, how children raced up and down the ladders of the mud-walled homes, the girls as boisterous as the boys.

In time he learned the complex chants for when the corn was planted and for when it took root and grew and tasseled. He learned the prayers and the myths of how the world was created and how kachinas carried messages. He was invited to ceremonies where non-Indians had never been. He was inducted into the Sacred Order of the Bow and given the name of Medicine Flower—Te-na-tsa-li—which children liked to shout at him on the streets. On long trips by mule, his first experiences in a saddle, he discovered ruins of early pueblos containing old tools and old baskets.

The rough outdoor life was hard for Cushing, for he had always been delicate. He'd weighed less than two pounds at birth and had been carried around on a silk cushion. As a youngster and still frail, he'd played in the woods alone, wearing the Indian costume he'd made for himself, talking to trees and looking for arrowheads.

Over the years he'd studied Indian things and written to people at the museum, pestering them for work. When he was offered a job without pay, he quit college to take it. He was then 18 and it was four years later that his chance came to go West. His instructions were to observe, record, and write back frequently, though no one knew then he'd stay on to become an Indian himself and even, as people said of him, to "out-Zuni the Zunis."

Museum people say today that Cushing may not have been so well accepted by the Indians as he claimed. The photographs *are* mildly funny: A skin-and-bones, half-naked man done up in kachina skirt and mask or laden with jewelry including earrings in his pierced ears.

But all his writings show the strong bond he felt with the Indians. Back East he'd tell the stories he had heard by firelight, when he and the boys and girls beside him had sat very tall. For it was known that anyone who slumped before the tale was told would grow crooked before growing old. He'd try to tell how, according to the Zunis, every person, every owl and every tree had a life of its own. And not only these had life, but everything that people made and wore and used, which is why bows and bowls and kachina dolls were to be cared for lovingly.

Ponder this, he would say to people, when you call the Indians "barbarians."

Allende Meteorites

ANYONE who's looked at an Allende meteorite can brag about having met the oldest thing anywhere—not the black rock itself, but the white fragments inside.

News of a huge meteorite shower at 1 A.M. of a winter's morning in 1969 set off a pair of museum men, Brian Mason and Roy Clarke, Jr., in a rush to investigate. They'd had word of the rackety sonic boom and the brilliant flash and had heard that rock fragments had scattered themselves in a broad path over the farmlands of Chihuahua, Mexico.

Every meteorite is exciting—"a poor man's space probe," Mason calls it, a prize from outer space. But these meteorites were extra exciting, for there were an astonishing lot of them, and it was clear from the start that they were a rare type. As the men drove into the town of Parral and glimpsed one large rock on show in the window of a newspaper office, they knew they were onto something big.

The following day, 36 schoolboys, an entire sixth grade, were let out of class to help with the search. Their directions from the museum men were to walk side by side in a line toward the foothills and, when they saw an out-of-the-ordinary black rock, to yell.

It was an almost-spring day. Some fields were plowed and some not, but the earth was mostly bare, showing here and there the local white, brown and yellow rocks.

Mexican schoolboys, who help in the search, found pieces of the Allende meteorite shower in fields by their school.

The first yell went up within minutes. Through the day there were others, alerting the men to come and photograph before anyone touched the rocks. There were six finds, from a 4 pounder the size of a grapefruit to a rock that weighed 20 pounds.

The men thanked the boys heartily. The boys thanked the men for springing them from school.

Such meteorites had been found before but very few and only very, very small ones. Near Pueblito de Allende so many meteorites were picked up by the boys and by others, it was possible to share them generously, to cut slices and send them around the world. Scientists in 37 labs were already geared up and waiting to run tests on the first moon rocks as soon as Apollo XI brought them back. Meanwhile they were happy to look at the meteorites.

Discoveries about Allende didn't come in a flash. "It takes minutes to identify a meteorite," says Mason. "It can take years to decipher it." But when reports returned one by one from the labs, and when pieces of information fit with other pieces, excitement grew. And 16 years later, it is growing still.

Now it is almost certain that the white bits—the CAIs, or calcium-aluminum inclusions—are even older than the black rock that surrounds them. The black itself is run-of-the-mill, older-than-earth, older-than-moon, 4.5-billion-year-old solar-system stuff. But the white is from time and space and stars beyond the solar system. The white is most likely interstellar dust from an exploding supernova, which may reveal, as nothing else can, the origins of the solar system.

"If we'd known then what we know now," says Mason, "that we'd learn more about the origins of the universe from Allende than from all the lunar rocks of the space program, we'd have told the boys: You made a giant step for cosmochemistry."

Not just the Mexican sixth graders, but other people too, have been generous with meteorites. One woman, though, from Sylacauga, Alabama, expected large amounts of cash in return. Her meteorite had crashed through the ceiling of her house, bounced off the radio, and whacked her on the thigh, bruising her painfully. The Air Force took it away briefly to check it out as a possible unidentified flying object. Her landlord disputed her claim that God intended her to have it. He said the rock was his.

The museum did want the break-and-enter meteorite as a crowd attractor but wouldn't meet Ann Hodges's price of $10,000. Mrs. Hodges was told that meteorites are like postage stamps. Some are rare. Most are common. And hers, except for its grand story, was a common one.

The museum bought instead a meteorite that fell close-by in the same shower and landed in a country lane. The farmer who found it had read in the paper about the woman's experience. So when his mule refused to walk past an odd black rock, the man guessed what the rock was. He sold it for $50—it's now on show—and he bought his mule the best meal it ever had.

Still other people send in meteorites-that-are-not-meteorites. Some 100 mail-ins come each year, and rarely is one the real thing. There used to be a drawer for them labeled MISTAKEN GEOLOGY. Now the gifts are mailed back.

Rejection letters have to be tactful. They begin, "There has been an understandable mistake," and go on to say, "You have sent a piece of slag" (the waste product in making steel). Or "You have sent a piece of iron." Or basalt. Or a pebble covered with plaster. Or hardened worm droppings.

People who see a flash in the sky are not apt to know the meteorite may land hundreds of miles away. They send along the first rock that looks odd to them, though meteorites with their black crusts don't look half so odd as some of the things people send.

One "meteorite" appeared on the sidewalk during a storm. A light flashed, wrote the sender, and then he saw a rock that wasn't there before. How to tell him the gritty object must have slipped off a shoe in the wet, the "inclusions" in it are sand, and his meteorite is a hard wad of chewing gum? This is no step for cosmochemistry, and the letter must say, "There has been an understandable mistake."

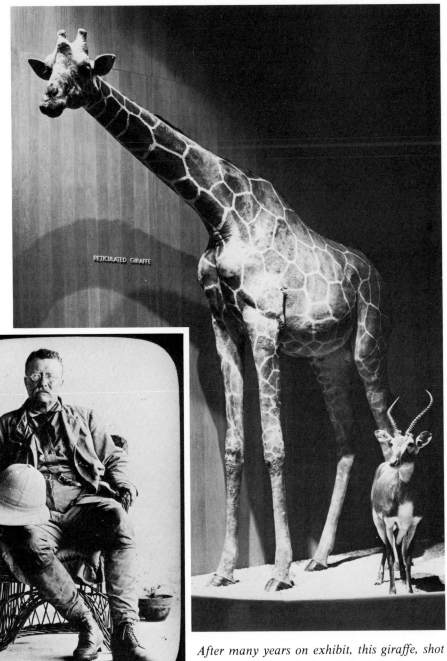

RETICULATED GIRAFFE

After many years on exhibit, this giraffe, shot by Teddy Roosevelt (inset), had rips in its skin that needed repair.

Reticulated Giraffe

THE reticulated giraffe isn't the one with the smudge spots but the one with white lines in a big pattern. Teddy Roosevelt shot it in 1909. He admired its fine proportions and its red-brown color.

As ex-President of the United States, he'd proposed to shoot big game in Africa and to bring back males, females and young for the museum, which had almost nothing African. No animal would be shot except for its use to science or for food. He said there'd never be such a chance again to collect. And his offer was accepted. With him he took his son Kermit, age 20, as photographer, and three men from the museum, though the men had to promise they'd leave the shooting to him.

Scrappy outdoorsman T.R. did things in a big way. His equipment lists for the trip, filed away at the museum, include multitudes of traps, vast amounts of ammunition, a mountain of salt (four tons for treating skins), and many kinds of knives (including shoemakers' tools for working around hoofs), cans of Boston baked beans by the case, ten pairs of eyeglasses (for he was lost without them), his own canvas bathtub, a little library of books (among them *The Luck of Roaring Camp, Huckleberry Finn* and *Alice's Adventures in Wonderland*) and numbers of tents. His own tent was green, and he took along an American flag to fly from it.

The safari began with a train ride through a park teeming with

American flag marked the ex-President's tent at camp.

game, where T.R. sat above the locomotive's cowcatcher and got his first look at flocks of exotic birds and at giraffes running alongside the tracks. At the end of the ride his little army of porters, 260 strong, greeted him with cheers of "Jambo Bwana King Ya Amerik" ("Hello, Mister King of America").

Roosevelt rode horseback for days on end. Over grassy plains that reminded him of the American West he tracked animals and observed and shot. By night, having bathed in a hot tub, he'd sit outside his tent hearing the songs of porters and the barks of nearby zebras. And he'd write in his journal, rewriting and re-rewriting, till his pages looked like patchwork.

The expedition brought back 512 big game animals and ten times as many small animals, reptiles, plants, fish. In Washington, even before the unpacking, people flocked to see the pileups of barrels and crates on the Mall outside the museum. Later they marveled to see the skins, mounted, on exhibit, for this was a time before fine nature movies were made in the wild, and the sight of the animals was a rare treat.

To this day, to the left and right of the giraffe stand the "Bully" president's lions, his wart hogs, his rhinos (which always looked

A team of porters helped with camp chores, the hunt and preparing specimens.

stupid and truculent to him with their little pig eyes) and his zebras
and storks and cranes and ostriches.

In his book, *African Game Trails*, T.R. tells how he missed the
first giraffe he shot at. The animal was so huge he thought it nearer
to him than it was, and his bullet fell short. Another giraffe, which
he caught napping, asleep standing up, disappeared at a gambol
when it saw it was watched.

No other animal, T.R. said, is so striking looking as the giraffe.
None has such a curious gait, a kind of rocking-horse gallop with
both hind legs coming forward at once outside the forelegs. And no
animal is harder to approach unseen, for the long-necked beasts
always have a fine high view.

Now 75 years have passed, and the giraffe T.R. finally caught
has undergone repairs. The man who attends to it wishes the skin
had been better tanned. It was never really tanned at all, not to
shoe-leather softness. It was only pickled. And its stiffness causes
problems.

Recently he did a major fix-up of 24 large rips. He did it right
in the Mammals hall with passersby offering suggestions. First he
"relaxed" the torn giraffe skin by applying damp rags to it. Then

Dust is a menace to animals that stand free, out from under glass. Dust flies in through the doors. It's tracked in on shoes. Drafts blow it about, along with fuzz from people's coats and lint from their jeans. The grittiness gives animals a dingy look, damaging fur and skin.

One official dust chaser, wearing a backpack vacuum machine, makes rounds of the halls from animal to animal pushing

he put glue between the skin and the mannequin inside it using a paintbrush or, in tight places, a hypodermic needle. And then, while the glue dried, he held the hide flat by nailing on cardboard strips like giant bandages.

His patch work was a success, but it left cracks an inch wide where pieces of skin no longer met. These he filled with a goo of beeswax and balsam and oil paint. He spread it on warm and then ran a comb over it to give a hairy look. As a last step he repainted his cart of equipment. To keep the leaping Indian tiger sleek, he vacuums its thick fur Mondays and Fridays using the upholstery attachment. The elephant, on the other hand, is *supposed* to look dusty. In the wild it gives itself dust baths. So the museum's master cleaner spruces it up only twice a year.

The technique is to wave a feather duster near the animal's skin without actually touching it and then to catch the dust in motion with the vacuum nozzle. With skeletons the trick is to keep from snagging the duster in a crack and leaving a feather behind. Such a feather has to be worked loose with sticky tape on a long stick.

Frank Braisted, the animals' cleaner, always reports bad news fast: moth eggs under the saddle of the South American cowboy's pony, or a claw missing from a polar-bear paw, or a whisker from the tiger (whose muzzle now bristles with half natural whiskers and half fiberglass substitutes).

Equipment matters. Braisted favors soft diapers for wiping down the life-size plastic whale model and the papier-mâché *Stegosaurus* and for polishing glass eyeballs. He wants ostrich feathers in his dusters to be black. Gray ones scratch.

the hair to its original colors. He was glad he'd taken *before* photographs to go by. A wrong line or two on the face and he could have changed this giraffe to a different species.

He was glad, too, to see that, overall, the animal has kept its fine red-brown color. Giraffes scarcely fade, unlike zebras, whose black stripes go gray and need touch-ups with paint or with do-it-yourself hair dye from the drugstore.

Edward Nelson (left) and the exhibit based on a photograph he took of a kayaking seal hunter.

Bering Sea Eskimo

THE Eskimo in the gut-skin parka has been throwing his seal spear, or about to throw it, for more years than anyone remembers. He's hunting from his kayak. And the weather must be fair. He has bare hands. No gloves, no mittens. He's wearing his pants with the fur side out instead of winter style, fur side in. And his parka hangs down loose. In rough weather he'd tie its skirt around the cockpit to keep out water.

The scene copies an old photograph. Edward Nelson took the picture on a flat-calm day 100 years ago. And then, as he was instructed to do, he went about collecting everything he'd recorded on his glass-plate negative. He got the harpoon and the coils of seal-skin cord and the curious float (it looks like a toy seal but it's a real seal's skin puffed up like a balloon) and the visor that protects against glare and the wonderfully waterproof, see-through parka made of ribbony strips of seal intestines. And of course the kayak. He shipped everything short of the man inside the clothes to Washington.

Nelson's job, when he was sent to St. Michael, Alaska, was to record weather for the U.S. Army Signal Corps and to make a study of the life around him. He was 24 and interested in everything. He knew a lot about birds and nothing about Alaska, except that the people of the Bering Sea, where he'd be, were not whalers and not

Painted from bow to stern along the kayak's side is the dragon-like *palraiyuk*, which Nelson noticed appeared on most Bering Sea kayaks. The long skinny *palraiyuks* were monsters of powerful evil. They lurked in the marsh, snatching men from their kayaks and women from the shore where they drew water, and devouring them. The painted image on boats, Nelson was told, protected the

igloo builders. They lived on marshy tundra, hunting seals and catching birds and fish.

In four years' time, he came to know them well. And because he was so curious and eagerly bought and traded for the most surprising things, not precious furs, but ordinary, everyday used tools, toys and half-worn-out boots, the people were curious about him, too. Though children ran shrieking to their mothers at their first sight of a white man, the parents welcomed him.

boat and the seal hunter and his wife from such attack. It even protected the seal in the sea. For seal, boat, man and woman were bound, one to the other, in a special harmony.

The hunter believed that every seal had a spirit like his own. If the seal were killed in a manner showing it respect, then the spirit—which lived on after death—would choose to dwell in the body of a newborn animal. And game would be plentiful.

Into the kayak, the hunter built a kind of magic, giving the boat, too, a spirit. Under the cockpit rim, out of sight, he tied two charms, one with a man's face, one with a woman's. On a little ivory knob on deck, which kept his paddle from slipping, he carved the features of a sea parrot, who lived by hunting at sea; and on the spearpoint, the features of a winged creature who flew true. These would keep him safe on the water and bring him good fortune. Around the rim of the cockpit and around the rim of his visor, he gouged a lifeline to hold the spirit within. He painted the line the spirit-life color, blood red.

The boat he built with the help of his wife, who stitched the sealskin cover, was light and maneuverable. It was also handsome—to honor and comfort the animals on which his life depended.

Once when he entered a crowded lodge during a gift-giving festival, a woman called out, to shouts of laughter from the others, "Where is the man who buys good-for-nothing things?" and tossed him little presents. Her name for him stuck and became a friendly greeting.

In all, Nelson collected 10,000 things. Some were butterflies he caught in his hat. Some were mosses the Eskimos used for diapers. Some were birds' eggs, which he got by lowering himself over a

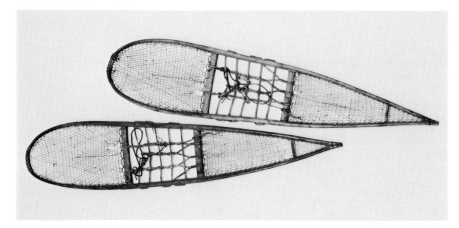

Nelson's snowshoes.

precipice on a rope while rocks rained down past him. He traded buttons and cloth and axe blades for fishhooks made by the Eskimos, and for the little ivory cord attachers with which they lashed equipment to the deck of the kayak. He also collected their sewing kits, called "housewives," some of which were made from caribous' ears; some were carved from ivory.

The steps that went into making each thing greatly interested Nelson. He wrote down how ivory was soaked in urine to soften it before it was carved; how grass was twined to make it into boot socks; and how the seal gut was split and dried and folded so that no stitches pierced all the layers of the parka at once, and no water could leak through the needle holes.

The long trips Nelson made were rough and dangerous. He went by dogsled and kayak, lugging his bulky camera and specimens. To the pair of snowshoes he gave the museum he attached a note: he'd logged 1800 miles wearing them. He braved rains, sleet, fog, winds, ice; slept night after night in freezing wet or in the half-thawed muck in a lodge. Sometimes his Eskimo hosts, seeing him chilled and exhausted, would take a turn wearing his clothes to dry them with their body heat.

A letter he wrote in 1879 tells of a storm he was lucky to survive. He was returning from a collecting trip with a cargo of 17 emperor geese, riding in a 3-cockpit kayak. When the storm hit, water sloshed in and great waves prevented a landing. Ashore at last, at the mouth of the Pikmiktalik River, Nelson had lost the use of his legs and had to be lifted out and set, stiff, on the beach. He thawed somewhat by a fire, he wrote, then hung out his clothes to dry and stalked about bare. While he was reviving, a little bird with a nest nearby entertained him. She seemed not at all alarmed to be caught and studied. Nelson released her and did not take her eggs either, "for it seemed a pity to rob such a confiding creature."

What the great collector collected from this drenching was a new respect for seal-gut clothing. He wouldn't have gotten so wet if he'd worn his parka.

Team of model makers poses in the "magic shop" with the pterosaur just before it was hung—to fly over the dinosaurs.

Pterosaur

THE pterosaur hangs over the heads of the dinosaurs, glaring down at them. Not a dinosaur, not a bird or a bat, but a flying reptile, it has a beaky head, a snake's neck and a wingspread, wingtip to wingtip, as wide as a four-lane highway.

This life-size model was made by model makers—people in the "magic shop" who turn out real-looking trees for a rain forest exhibit, vines, fruit and one-of-a-kind things like a shark's jaw or an Ice-Age mannequin. Odd jobs come their way, and this pterosaur, they say, was the oddest and the hardest. It had to be strong enough not to droop or buckle and light enough not to pull down the ceiling.

In 1972 there'd been an exciting find in west Texas: the fossil skeleton of a pterosaur—new genus, new species, more than twice the size of any known before. People said, "Where but in Texas?...." It was named *Quetzalcoatlus* (for a serpentine Aztec god) *northropi* (for the Northrop Flying Wing bomber).

The skeleton wasn't complete, but paleontologists, "reading" the pieces of wing and neck, jaw, thigh and beak, could pretty well tell what the pterosaur looked like and how it lived and flew. They passed along their guesses and all that they knew to the magic shop. Then it was up to the model makers to design such a creature and build it.

"We puzzled it out," says one of the men. "At the start we were thinking *monster* because of the hugeness. In life this pterosaur stood eyeball-to-eyeball with the giant *Diplodocus*. Even in pieces it would crowd us out of our biggest workrooms. But then we began to think *butterfly*.

"Here we were, carving wing bones that were seven and a half feet long, longer than a giraffe's leg bones. The real pterosaur had wing bones that were strong but hollow. They were more air than bone, and their walls were thinner than a chalk line. We were working on the largest animal that ever flew, but in life it weighed maybe 75 pounds, half what I do.

"So incredibly light and with such huge wings! We pictured it at take-offs: the wings at first tucked behind, like an Englishman's umbrella; then, opened out, catching a breeze. And, poof! It flew! Airborne, it rode the currents and the updrafts. Our pterosaur could flap—the muscle power shows in the fossils—but it was a soaring animal and an effective one at that, we're told. It soared, scarcely moving a wing. It stayed up practically forever. And it dove when it spied fish in the shallows.

"The monster image had thrown us off. We were really building a sailplane, using a plane's long, slim framework and light materials and giving it the features of an animal. Once we caught on, we knew what to do!"

Not counting the messing-about time and the thinking, the work took two years. A lot of clay play came at the start, with little models to test out shapes and positions; then a bigger model; then at last the full-size flyer, which turned the shop into a hangar as a team of ten men and women welded and carved and painted and made rubber molds and fiberglass casts.

The scientists came by every so often, checking. They'd say "yes" to the twist of the neck and "yes" to the pose with wings set

40

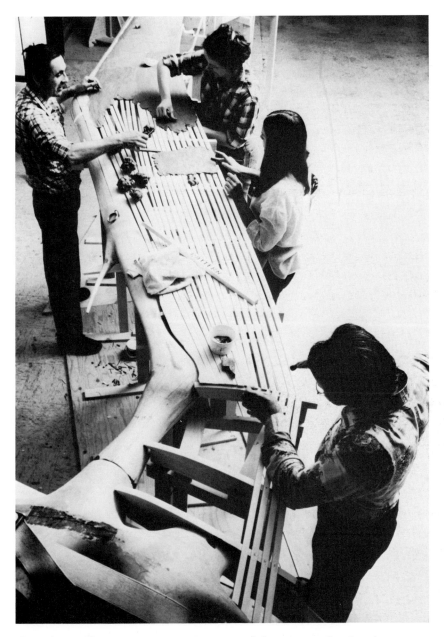

Carved wing bones are a permanent part of the pterosaur's wing, but the wood-slat framework was temporary—for shaping the fiberglass wing skin.

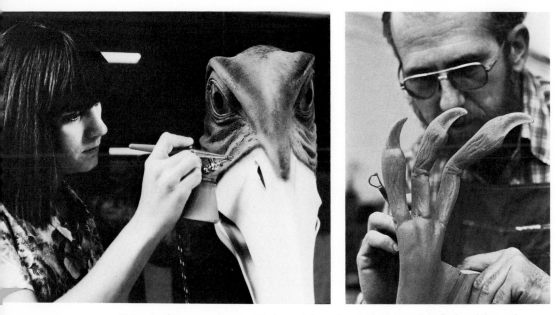

Scientists' best guesses guided model makers as they painted the skin and sculpted pterosaur fingers.

for a diving turn and "no" to a fish dangling from the beak. The fish would work for the model but not for the animal itself. One six-pound fish would throw this flyer off balance.

For everything there had to be a reason: for the fit of the bite and for the bulge by the eyes. Everything had to fit with the evidence. On the other hand the evidence had great gaps in it. Wingspan could have been 35 feet or 57 feet or any number of feet in between. The paleontologists chose 40 feet because of the 60-foot width of the hall of dinosaurs.

Colors had to be guesses because colors are not preserved in fossils. On the theory that most large animals are mud colored and that animals moving through the air tend to be darker up top than below, the shop crew chose brown for the skin, shading to light buff on the underbelly. They chose sulfur yellow with blood red splashes for the eyes.

The tongue was a guess. Its curves and pointy tip were copied from medieval dragons. Furriness for the body was something of a gamble. A pterosaur was not a bird or even the ancestor of a bird. It was not feathery. But furry? Some scientists think it was. Some think not. The museum's Nicholas Hotton, paleontologist and reptiles expert, has strong doubts. All the same he voted for fur.

"A model has to look plausible," he says. "A naked pterosaur looks like a flying sausage. It needs some texture." He agreed to the fur for the look of it. And so a model maker who was once a tailor fitted on a fake fuzz-fur coat, not to the wings, but to the body.

The finished *Quetzalcoatlus northropi* is something of an engineering masterpiece. All the hollow steel framework is hidden, covered with balsa wood carved in the shape of wing bones. With light shining from above, only the bone shapes show through the skin part of the wing. The effect is eerie.

It is as the makers intended, but they can't help wondering: if a complete skeleton is found someday, what will it show about their accuracy? Which clues did they read right? How badly did they blunder? If the model has to be altered, they say they wouldn't mind. They've missed the fierce-looking pterosaur (nickname Terry, gender female) and would welcome her back for an overhaul.

Rare blue Hope diamond glitters in its diamond necklace even though it's seen in dim light and through thick glass.

Hope Diamond

G UARDS say the second-most-asked question at Natural History is where to find the Hope diamond. (Most-asked: "Where's the bathroom?") At holiday time there are long lines to see it—the jumbo gem with its deep blue dazzle and its razzle-dazzle stories, some of which are bogus.

True are the stories about one owner, how extravagant she was and generous. Washingtonian Evalyn McLean was the kind of person who ran out of money on her Paris honeymoon even though she and her husband were each given $100,000 (value today: $1.5 million) by their fathers for spending. It was 3 years later, in 1911, that she bought the Hope diamond in its diamond-studded necklace (price $180,000).

She wore it often and for a double dazzle she'd hang a huge pear-shaped diamond from a hook at the base of the setting. She also wore the necklace around the house and when it felt heavy she'd take it off—and forget where she'd left it. After school her children and their friends would join her at turning over pillows and plunging hands down the gaps in overstuffed chairs till the lost was found.

A son teethed on the Hope diamond, and the Great Dane, Mike, wore it as a collar. Brides borrowed it, and, when Evalyn McLean visited the veterans' hospital, soldiers tossed her necklace from bed to bed.

It was New York jeweler Harry Winston who bought the necklace after her death and gave it to the museum in 1958. He mailed it in ordinary brown wrapping paper as if to say, "Here come some beetles," but he insured the package for $1 million.

These stories are true. The one about the stone's being stolen from the eye of an Indian idol is not. Nor is the story of a curse whereby tragic fates are supposed to befall the owners. The Paris jeweler who sold her the diamond knew Mrs. McLean thought unlucky things brought her good luck, and he played up the rumored curse as a sales pitch.

The real mystery is whether the Hope diamond is the French Blue, stolen from the French crown jewels. If it is, then its life has been one of high adventure. This much is known about the French Blue:

The stone was mined in India and sold in 1669 to Louis XIV, the "Sun King" of France. To make it more brilliant, he had it recut, bringing it down from 112 to 67 carats, and he wore it around his neck on a ribbon. After him, Louis XV had the gem set into a decoration called The Order of the Golden Fleece, which had a white diamond, a ruby, and the blue diamond in a line, with a gold sheep dangling below them.

At the time of the French Revolution, the crown jewels (taken from Louis XVI and Marie Antoinette) were kept in a building in Paris where citizens could come to look at them on certain days. A thief named Paul Miette, noticing that the building was poorly guarded, scaled the wall with some friends one September night in 1792 and forced a window. Once inside, the men fixed seals on the courtyard doors as if, by a judge's order, the building was not to be entered. And they filled their pockets with jewels.

The thieves returned two nights later, again up the wall, and nightly thereafter with ever more accomplices. Paris pawnbrokers reported strange goings-on, offers to them of surprisingly fine gems. But police checking the building saw the seals and said all must be well. By the end of the week some 50 people, half of them women friends of the thieves, were supping in the building by candlelight and roistering and throwing jewelry over the balcony to other friends below. One man fell to the street while climbing down. As police were arresting him, another fell on top of the first. Three officials of the building arrived to investigate, but in a case of mistaken identity *they* were taken by the police for questioning.

It was not until the next morning that the looting was discovered. By that time a trail of dropped jewels and empty settings led from the building to the river. The Order of the Golden Fleece with its blue diamond was not seen again in France.

A gap of 20 years falls between the cops-and-robbers games and the time in 1812 when an extraordinary blue diamond, its origin unknown, appeared in the hands of a London jeweler. It was large, 45 carats, but not nearly so large as the 67-carat French Blue. Seventeen years later Henry Hope listed it in the catalog of his gem collection. Was it the French Blue, recut to disguise it? Or was it a new gem entirely and not from the Golden Fleece? Hope listed a second blue diamond, a small one, which might also have come from the recutting, but it was later sold and lost track of.

At the museum much detective work has been done, but the puzzle of identity remains unsolved. One finding is that when the Hope is put under ultraviolet light it phosphoresces crimson—like a hot coal. Few blue diamonds exist. They come from a single mine. Some phosphoresce blue-green. If Hope's small one turned up and if it, too, glowed crimson, then the case would be even stronger— for Hope–French Blue.

Ten years ago the gem was briefly removed from its necklace for new tests. On its own and out of its great bank vault of a showcase (where lights are dim to keep the gem from overheating), the Hope glinted and winked—deep blue and steely blue and lavender. Then it was also seen that, while it is flawless, it is a "stressed" stone, the kind that is easily shattered just from the way it is formed.

Of course it was handled with care, a blanket held under it at each move. Still, as the gem went from hand to hand, an awful thing happened. It fell on the floor and bounced. The man who crawled under the table to fetch it reappeared with both fists closed, asking, "Which half shall I show you first?" Then (no one was laughing), he quickly opened his hands—one empty, one holding the still-perfect diamond.

Rift Worm

*R*iftia pachyptila Jones is a whopping, pasty-looking worm, as big around as a garden hose, floating upright in a bottle. It has a collar up top and, like a bottle brush, a plume of tentacles. In life the plume was red but here it's a no-color color as ghostly as the rest. The worm is even more peculiar than it looks. It has no mouth and no gut—no way, or so it seems, to take in food or digest it.

The worm was collected by a mechanical claw, which reached out from the submersible ship *Alvin* and grabbed it. The *Alvin* was nearly two miles down in total darkness, where the ocean floor was expected to be barren. But when the sub's lights were switched on, they lit up a helter-skelter of animals. There were clams as big as dinner plates and jellyfish like dandelions and worms like this one, in clumps and tangles, waving their plumes and undulating.

The *Alvin*'s crew were investigating the rift in the sea floor near the Galapagos Islands in the Pacific. They were finding little pockets teeming with animals. This one they called the Rose Garden. The water here was different. Gushing up from deep down under, it was hot, heated by volcanoes, while the ocean all around was near freezing. It was also different chemically. It had almost no oxygen and was loaded with sulfides. Although sulfides usually poison animals, here animals were thriving—outlandishly. It was all baffling, which is why the worms were sent to worms specialist Meredith Jones at the museum.

Jones was bowled over by their size. One of the worms is five feet long. He was impressed by the stiff casings that cover the soft bodies. And by the plumes. He figures each one is a bundle of 250,000 little feathery threads. But what amazed him most was the no-mouth, no-gut situation. How does this worm keep itself alive and grow and reproduce? Some food could come in through the plume and some through the thin body wall, but what food is there where sunlight never penetrates and the water is loaded with poisons?

In his lab, surrounded by large pale forms in jars, Jones kept looking at the worms, and thinking, and cutting thin sections (he calls them his baloney slices) to look at under microscopes that magnify 30,000 times. The more he looked at the worms, the more curious they seemed. Their insides were different from anything he'd seen in a lifetime.

A lot of granular stuff filled the body all up and down—a sort of mush, like ground-up liver. And it had tiny yellow flecks in it. Thinking about sulfides in the water, Jones was sure there was a connection between them and the flecks. A minerals man down the hall said yes, the flecks were pure yellow sulfur.

Though he still had a lot to understand, Jones gave a show-and-tell presentation to other worms people. A student in the audience told him she thought the mush stuff must be bacteria. She was working in marshes, and it seemed to her that bacteria were breaking down sulfur compounds in the marsh water and producing energy from them.

It was just the clue Jones needed. Bacteria inside the worm's body, he found, are doing the same thing. Bacteria by the billions

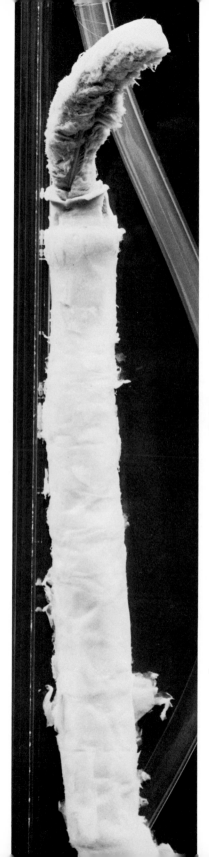

*In his lab Meredith Jones shows off a
five-foot rift worm, which is even longer
than the one on exhibit (left).*

are the mush. They live in the worms and nourish them. Jones isn't entirely sure how. Maybe, like certain ants, they harvest crops, taking them from the water for the worm. Maybe the worm feeds directly on dead and dying bacteria or on material the bacteria excrete. At any rate the worm owes its life to the bacteria and to the sulfides.

For almost every other animal in the world, even for other animals that never see sunlight, the source of energy—through plants—is the sun. For this plumed worm and its sea-bottom neighbors the source of energy is a deep-down volcano, gushing "poisons." As underwater discoveries go, this was the most important of the century.

Twice now, Jones has made the dive in *Alvin* to find his rift worm. He says the dives weren't as exciting as he'd imagined. After seeing the worms in *National Geographic Magazine* and on television, seeing them in their Rose Garden was an anticlimax. "I just thought, 'By George, there they are, my worms!' "

The dive took an hour and a half for a mile-and-a-half trip, and there was no sensation like going down in an elevator because the cabin was pressurized. When the *Alvin* reached the Rose Garden, it stayed seven hours while Jones, scrunched down, watched out of the floor-level portholes and the claw collected.

Since that time Jones's rift worms have been found at 4 other hot-water pockets. And he has seen 6 different kinds. It will take many more years of work to understand them. He thinks 15.

For now it is certain: the odd worm is a new family, new genus, new species. Its scientific name is *Riftia* for where it lives, *pachyptila* from the Greek words meaning thick and feather, Jones for the fellow who opened this can of worms and is puzzling out its secrets.

As for the worm on exhibit, Jones had so few to work with, it was a pity to give one up even for people to look at. He slit his show worm open, saved all the insides for his lab, filled up the worm with cotton, and stitched it shut again—as anyone can see by going around behind it.

Freeze drying the eight-foot Komodo dragon for exhibit was a challenge the freeze-dry expert says he does not wish to meet again.

Komodo Dragon

THE Komodo dragon, 8 feet long from snout to tip of whiplash tail, looks like the storybook dragon that belched fire and smoke. Komodos, though, are real—great heavyset hunting lizards that live in Indonesia and make a meal out of deer or wild pigs. For five years this one lived at the National Zoo, where its snapping jaws, its claws and its sheer size (238 pounds) attracted a lot of attention.

The zoo director got the dragon in 1964 on a visit to Indonesia. He was sipping tea with the head of the government when he was asked what animals he'd take home if he had his wishes. He thought he ought to sound modest, not grabby, so he named a few little birds and then he thought, why not blurt out that his heart's desire was a pair of Komodos? He did and his wish was granted.

The night before his departure from Indonesia, the Komodos were in their crates in the walled garden of the U.S. Embassy. Or rather, the female was in hers. The male had chewed through a rope and escaped and was hissing in the shrubbery. The young Marine on guard duty had his hand on the trigger of his .45 and was prepared to shoot.

Though dragons were a novelty to the zoo man, he knew a thing or two about crocodiles and how to handle them. He called for a broom and then he started sweeping. "A broom," he says now,

When buffalo, goats, porcupines and tortoises lived in pens on the Mall beside the museum in the nineteenth century, scientists and taxidermists could watch them right out their windows. Here chief taxidermist William Temple Hornaday strolls on the grass with a buffalo calf he captured in Montana in 1886.

In time the close-at-hand collection of creatures became too numerous and too smelly, and a buffalo bull calf almost gored a nursemaid. Then special park land was found for the National Zoo, which is where the Komodo dragon lived, a gift to the American people.

calmly, "is a nice tool for moving an animal. He won't break his teeth, and the feel of it is something he's not sure of. It lets a person keep his distance, too." On this occasion some pushes at the shoulder swept the dragon into its crate. The zoo man told the Marine he deserved a medal. "It was the bravest thing I ever saw—your *not* shooting."

At the zoo, people liked the Komodos, who moved about in a sluggish way except at mealtimes, when they put on bursts of speed and ripped into chunks of meat, thrashing them about and choking down skin and bones. When the animals died, zoo-goers were sad. It was some consolation to send this one, the male, over to the freeze-dry lab at Natural History to be preserved.

The Komodo dragon was the most difficult animal the lab ever worked on. Because of its tough skin it took longer than any other creature to lose its moisture. Nine months it spent in the vacuum tank, crowding out a peacock and bobcats who were waiting turns.

The curve of the tail is realistic for a Komodo, but it also had to be just as you see it to fit in the tank. The eyes, as with all freeze-dried animals, are fake. These are ready-mades, intended for a mountain goat. They're greenish yellow with an oval pupil—just right for a Komodo once they're turned sidewise.

The good thing about freeze-dried animals is that they keep their innards and their life-like good looks. The bad thing is that they make a picnic for predators. Rodents loose in the museum have been known to gnaw at a freeze-dried fox and carry away a chipmunk from a little woodland exhibit as if it were a gift of jerky. The dragon is kept behind glass to protect it.

Sea creature Sidneyia inexpectans *(shown approximately life-size) lived 300 million years before dinosaurs appeared on earth.*

Sidneyia Inexpectans

Sidneyia inexpectans is a little sea creature unlike any other and is almost three times older than the first dinosaurs. It's nothing special to look at. People never ask guards "Where's *Sidneyia?*" or crowd around it. They mostly go right past.

If they do catch a glimpse, they may not be sure what they saw. *Sidneyia* is shiny black, like carbon paper, and the rock in which it's preserved is dull black. What shows, black-on-black, is a little body, bulgy up front. It's marked off in segments and has stubby, jointed legs and whiskers.

The freakish thing about it is that it survived. And that, freakishly, someone found it.

At the end of summer, 1909, Charles Doolittle Walcott was approaching Kicking Horse River pass in the Canadian Rockies. He was a geologist who'd spent his summer collecting fossil-bearing rocks. And he was on his way back to the museum with a heavily laden pack train when he saw a block of fallen rock on the trail. Walcott jumped down from his horse to move the rock out of the animal's way. But first, from habit, he gave it a few whacks with his hammer and split it.

What he saw amazed him. The rock had fossils in it of little sea creatures, not the kind with hard shells, but soft squishy ones, which ordinarily are not preserved.

Walcott had to get back to Washington. All he could do at the time was climb above the trail till he found the seam from which the rock had fallen. The seam was only 18 inches thick and tapered—not long, not very deep. It would have been easy to miss. Walcott returned the next summer and for four more summers after, blasting out the rock with dynamite and hauling it down on his back. He quarried the lot of it, bringing back 35,000 slabs, some 100,000 specimens in all.

His find was a record of a kind of life no one knew existed, of lacy-looking creatures, and blobby ones, and some with eyes on stalks and all manner of spikes. Some were shrimplike, and some were crablike and some were like jellyfish or sponges. And most, *Sidneyia* among them, were not like anything that exists today, but just, at least to modern eyes, odd looking.

The animals had lived on the bottom of the sea, where a mud slide one day smothered them. The mud didn't crush them, but it kept air from rotting them and currents from rumpling them and predators from eating them. The mud slide caught them just as they were—swimming. And as mud hardened to shale, the swimmers were preserved.

In later upheavals the whole underwater layer of shale with the swimmers caught in it landed high on a mountainside. It started out where Montana is. And, with the heaving, it wound up in Canada. It might never have been noticed except that one chunk of it, 530 million years after the mudslide, fell on a trail. And of all the people in the world, Walcott was one of very few who would have known what to make of it.

Walcott was a famous geologist, and he was the head of the Smithsonian Institution. Yet when he told about his finds, other scientists thought he was joking and that he'd maybe faked the

60

photographs. Tentacles and eyeballs so perfectly preserved? Gills and guts all showing? Even the contents of guts? It wasn't till Walcott mailed out pieces that his colleagues were convinced—by seeing for themselves.

For two of his summers of quarrying, Walcott had his young sons with him to do camp chores and split rock. When Sidney, age ten, one day cracked a rock and showed its creatures to his father, Walcott told the boy he'd found a species new to science. "I didn't expect to do *that!*" said Sidney. And so the father named the species *Sidneyia inexpectans.*

Young Walcott's *Sidneyia* became a type specimen, written up and named in a scientific paper. From that time, all other creatures resembling it have been compared with the type in order to decide if they, too, are *Sidneyia.* How much like it are they? How different? As Natural History's most valuable possessions, type specimens rate special attention. That's why during World War II all type specimens, including Sidney's *Sidneyia,* were carried to caves (along with such treasures as the flag that inspired the "Star-Spangled Banner") in case of a wartime attack on Washington.

In the showcase, *Sidneyia* appears, as it did in the sea, with such companions as *Waptia,* which looks like a ball of wool with knitting needles stuck through it, *Opabinia,* with five eyes across its head, and *Hallucigenia,* which has seven pairs of stilt legs and seven pairs of tentacles with periscope extensions.

Now textbooks on fossils tell all about Walcott's find of the Burgess Shale, as his collection is called, and how important and irreplaceable it is. For without it as evidence, who would know that the sea once upon a time, in the Cambrian Age, teemed with such creatures as these, which flourished and then vanished?

Gilbert Islanders did battle wearing vine vests, spiky helmets and swords edged with sharks' teeth.

South Sea Suit of Armor

AN old suit of body armor from the South Seas has a tunic woven out of vines, also a spiky helmet of porcupine-fish skin and swords studded with sharks' teeth. It was peacefully traded, in 1841, for chewing tobacco, but a terrible incident followed, one of many for the U.S. Exploring Expedition.

The U.S. Ex Ex (so written on old labels) was as glorious an achievement for its time as a voyage to the moon is for ours. And the men on it—500 Navy men plus 8 young civilian scientists—performed heroic feats. In six sailing ships they circled the globe and crisscrossed the Pacific three times. They charted islands and made treaties with chiefs. They established that Antarctica is a continent. And, as they were charged to do by the U.S. Government, they collected an inventory of the world's plants and animals. Birds, bird-feather capes, lizards, fish, fish traps and corals—things never known or ever imagined—were gathered and brought to Washington. The men were gone four years, and their work brought honor to the nation. But they did not get a heroes' welcome on their return. So many mishaps and fights and bungles occurred from the start that the Exploring Expedition was also dubbed the Deplorable Expedition.

The events that took place in collecting the armor were deplorable indeed. When the ships anchored by one of the Gilbert

Islands, islanders came aboard, eager to trade. Not at the start but sometime after, they turned hostile. They showed in gestures, grimacing, how their swords could lop off heads and disembowel. In turn the seamen hoisted one of the new-bought suits of armor above the deck and shot at it. Their idea, which backfired, was to discourage fighting—to show how the tunic, though it protected against toothy swords, was easily penetrated by bullets.

At one point a seaman was kidnaped and murdered on the island. And when landing boats went ashore to negotiate, hundreds of the islanders lined the beach, lashing the sea with their swords and rocking the boats. Two chiefs, as they were rallying the warriors to attack, were shot. Twenty islanders were killed, their village burned.

The incident troubled men of the expedition. Some wished stinging mustard seed had been shot from the guns instead of bullets (a ploy that worked in a threatening situation in New Zealand). One of the goals of the expedition was to make friends with native peoples so that shipwrecked or stranded seamen would in the future be well treated. Here it had made enemies.

On the ships there was little good feeling. Navy men complained about the scientists all along the way. They were known as "scientifics," but the seamen often called them "clam diggers" and "bug catchers" and belittled their work. The scientists complained about the damp, dark, cramped little staterooms where they dissected and pickled and labeled their specimens, surrounded by their own wet clothes and gear. One, the scientist-artist Titian Peale, wrote home to his children that he was his own bootblack and washerwoman and his room was the size of their mother's bed.

Everyone complained about the rats and about the Captain, Charles Wilkes. A brilliant seaman and a petty tyrant, he paced the

Captain Charles Wilkes, commander of the U.S. Exploring Expedition.

decks, stern, secretive and aloof. Because he required the men to keep diaries for his inspection, one officer kept a second diary as well for his private remarks on the Captain. Wilkes's own narratives of the journey were read by Herman Melville when he was writing *Moby Dick.* A New Zealand chief became the model for the tattoed Queequeg in the novel, and Wilkes served as a model for the cruel, brooding Captain Ahab. On his return, Wilkes was publicly reprimanded for the whippings on board.

As for the collections, quite a lot of the objects never got back to Washington. Many were lost when one of the ships sank. Many were badly handled and damaged.

In all the confusion when the massive shipments arrived, people who didn't seem to know one end of a bird from the other, or male from female, put together the specimens in odd ways. One "helper" removed from hundreds of shellfish in jars all the identity tags with the numbers that were keyed to the scientist's drawings and notes. (The tags were discoloring the alcohol, so they were put in a separate jar!) Other helpers sawed off bows and arrows to fit them neatly into drawers.

Nothing bad happened to the armor, though. Swords, tunic and helmet, too prickly for handling, came through fine.

Fossil bones of flesh-eater Antrodemus *stride toward prey as* Antrodemus *did in life.*

Antrodemus

MEET *Antrodemus* 145 million years after his life. A skeleton of dark fossil bones, he has been caught in action, moving fast toward a meal, which for him is not leafy vegetation but a leaf-eating *Stegosaurus* almost as big as himself.

In 1979 when the hall of dinosaurs was remade, planners thought it needed something fierce. It needed gaping jaws and saw-teeth, a predator in action. The plant-eating dinosaurs are huge and strange looking, with spikes and great plates and horns, but they are not *doing* much of anything. A meat eater on the move would impress people.

Meat eaters are in short supply. Fewer of them lived, and because they lived in exciting and dangerous ways they tended to be damaged. By good fortune the museum had a fine specimen. And Arnold Lewis was the person to prepare it for exhibit.

He had two years, till the new hall opened, to clean up the bones and stand *Antrodemus* on his feet in a hunting position. As such work goes, two years is not much time. But Lewis was an old hand, and it helped to have a specimen in such good condition.

Most dinosaurs in museums are composites, put together from scraps, like cars from spare parts. This skeleton, though, had been a great find. It was practically complete. If the fossil hunters who quarried it in the 1880s in Colorado hadn't thrown the tail over the cliff (they thought it belonged to another animal), it would have been just about perfect.

The bones were amazingly hard, too, unlike most dinosaur bones, which are rotten, punky, crumbly. And they were easy to see because they were black and the rock they were imbedded in was a pale sand color. Most often the colors blend, and it is difficult to tell where the rock ends and the bone begins. Lewis knew he was lucky.

Part of the work had already been done. The skull and some bones had been freed from the rock back when the animal was first written up for scientific papers. Still, it took Lewis six months just to grind away rock from the remaining bones to see what he had. He used chisels and picks and power drills, and he proceeded with caution. If a tool slipped, he'd nick a bone or dent it or scratch it. If he dropped a pelvis bone, it would shatter like glass.

All along he was reading up on *Antrodemus* and looking at photographs and at an old drawing with the bones numbered 1 through 238 (not counting some 30 bones in the head). When an artist made him a new drawing to work from, it showed *Antrodemus* running, one leg lifted high. The pose was dramatic, just what the new hall needed, but too dramatic, Lewis thought. So did the dinosaur expert, Nicholas Hotton.

The men agreed. Lifted that high, the leg would have pulled out of its socket. They made cardboard cutouts based on the drawing. They moved the leg around with pins and lowered it a lot.

Antrodemus, said Hotton, was no runner, no jumper, but a strider. He'd read the information in the bones, as paleontologists do. *Antrodemus* was a powerful strider, moving out at a tilt like a chicken's. He kept his front legs at the ready for grabbing prey and holding it. As he strode, his hind legs swung back and forth like

Preparator Arnold Lewis fits a bracket for attaching Antrodemus's *skull to the skeleton.*

pendulums, like the legs of elephants. Fossil tracks found on the ground show footprints that are even and narrowly spaced—left, right, left, right. The prints also show that the tail was not dragged but held up as a mighty counterweight.

Lewis, with a rhinoceros-size chicken in mind, sawed a shape to size out of wood, matching it to the position of the cardboard cutout. Then he built a giant sandbox and piled up sand to support the bones while he laid them out. "Without it," he said, "I'd have

The life-size model of *Stegosaurus* has a crackled skin and a multitude of warty-looking lumps. It was made for the 1904 world's fair in St. Louis by a company in Milwaukee that specialized in candy boxes and party favors, and then it was shipped to the museum. Because of a rumor that the paper of its papiermâché innards is shredded dollar bills, people have long called it Moneybags. But when a couple of men from the U.S. Treasury Department checked out the rumor a few years back, they reported that the material isn't money at all. They'd scraped away a sample from a hind foot and analyzed it in their lab. It was plain old newspaper and glue. Some people at the museum still like to think that the model has a wad of $100 bills at its heart. But no one denies that it has one major flaw. In the series of great fan-shaped plates running down its spine, the largest should come *behind* the hips rather than in front. The modelmakers' guess was seen to be wrong when a *Stegosaurus* skeleton was later found intact. This model is such a beauty, though, no one thinks of pitching it out.

needed five hands." When the bones of the neck were joined, they formed a kind of half circle. Once all such curves and angles were established, Lewis could bend his steel for the framework and start attaching bones to it, lifting and lowering the largest of them with chain hoists hung from a ceiling beam.

In life the animal balanced, seesaw fashion, across the hips. Much of the front part was hollow with lungs and such. And the back was weighted with muscle. But without the meat, the skeleton is front-heavy, so the frame has to make up for it. The frame carries the weight. Yet it has to be almost out of sight so that people seeing the dinosaur will marvel at it and not at museum handiwork.

There was of course the matter of the missing tail. Lewis had to copy one. He made a rubber mold from a tail in a Utah museum and then cast a new tail by pouring plastic into the mold. He replaced ribs, all but five or six of which were splintered, some in hundreds of pieces. He hung the all right ribs, then tied on wires for the missing ones and built them up with fiberglass tape and with papier-mâché. Trickiest to reconstruct was the belly armor, the ribby bit that floats free without a backbone connection. Lewis kept it light, attached to the nearest ribs.

The one piece of guesswork was the sternum, or breast bone. The real bone existed, but it was shattered, and there was none to copy that was reasonably intact. "In such a quandary," Lewis says, "you go to other dinosaurs that walked on two feet. You check them out and their closest living relatives, too, which happen to be croco- diles." In the end he took his design from the sternum of a crocodile. As a friend in the lab says, "Sometimes Arnie has to hum a few bars and hope he gets it right."

Once done, the patching looked spotty. Lewis then painted the pipes and all his homemade pieces. He did not try for the closest match but purposely kept his paint lighter than the black of the bones. He was going by the museum's six-foot–six-inch rule. At a distance of six feet, the difference between real bones and fakes ought not to hit people in the eye. Close up, at six inches, if it can't be seen at all, then people are being tricked.

Lewis met his deadline. He'd put in two full years of brain work and muscle work, of heaving and hauling and delicate, close work, too. He'd used all his expertise in bones and stones and his skills at sculpting, painting, welding. And he was done on time.

Now at least once a week, sometimes still in his blue denim apron, splotched from fossil work in progress, he comes from his lab to look at *Antrodemus.* He thinks about the lunging tilt and the leg lift that puzzled him so long and about all the nicks and bumps on bones, which came, he thinks, from fights, and the big deformity on the collar bone, from a serious injury.

When someone in the crowd says, "*Antrodemus* was a tough customer," Lewis is the first to agree.

House-Mouse Mandible

A house-mouse mandible is a spiky little jawbone not half the size of a shirt button. From the looks of it, it's nothing a family would come from Sioux Falls, Iowa, to see. Yet here it is, on exhibit, at the start of the hall of Western Civilization, which moves along to impressive things like mummies and mosaics and cups from Troy.

It is here as a scrap of evidence. Sometime between 8,000 and 7,000 B.C. the people at Tepe Ganj Dareh, in Iran, shifted their lifestyle from wandering to staying put. Earlier, when they were on the move for food, they'd camped at the site, in spring, in summer. Now they settled in to live year-round. They built in a serious way, raised grain, and stored it indoors over the winter till the next year's planting. And mice moved into the grain bins, nibbling.

When the site was dug ten years ago, almost no mouse bones were found in the lowest layers of dirt, where the camps had been. Hundreds of mouse bones, including this one, were found inside the mud-brick house walls in upper layers. The sharp increase marked the people's shift to farm life and the beginnings of a house-mouse partnership with people.

Since that time the house mouse has gone far—wherever people are, and free meals. It has migrated all across Asia, Africa, Europe, to Britain by the Middle Ages, and then, by boat, in grain

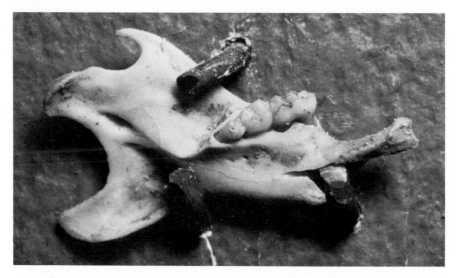

Lower left jawbone, greatly enlarged, of a middle-aged desert-dwelling house mouse.

sacks, to the New World. The Trans-Siberian railroad has given it lifts across the steppes, and airplanes have landed it in Australia and beyond. Of all the animals, only people are more widely spread about the globe than it is.

For the exhibit any part of the mouse could have been used, but the jawbone won the place of honor because mouse experts are great fanciers of teeth. They say a tooth, even just one, is the best indicator there is of the animal it belonged to, better by far than a hunk of fur or a foot, and they'd a lot rather have a molar than an incisor.

In this case, if even a little dot of one molar were all that remained, such an expert could be pretty sure that the animal was a mouse (not a shrew or a mole) and not just any mouse but a house mouse and specifically one belonging to the species called *Mus domesticus.* With the whole jawbone to go by, he'd be certain. For the first molar is bigger than the other two put together (a dead giveaway for *Mus domesticus*), *and* the cusps on its chewing surface (the little pointy mounds) are arranged in a pattern of three to the first row, three to the second, and two to the third.

An expert would be able to say, too, that this mouse had not been an old grandfather. It hadn't lived to be a year old (which is old for a house mouse), or even half a year, but more like two or three months. There's a middling amount of wear on the teeth, but, allowing for the sand in a desert mouse's diet, which wears down teeth extra fast, he'd put his guess at younger than middle age.

For such close scrutiny it helps to have a flashlight in hand. The hall of Western Civilization is dimly lit. And it helps to be a good squinter. The small mammals expert, Charles Handley, Jr., claims to have $\times 5$ eyes, which magnify like a microscope's, but it may just be that he's had a lot of practice.

Practice comes from years out in the field and from work with the collection. In the rodent range, a room as long as a city block, 54 drawers hold 75 house mice each, their bodies side by side in rows, fur plumped out with cotton, skulls arranged close by. It takes a batch at least as large as this to map the mouse migrations and to see the variations in color and in size. House mice from cold climates are bigger than those from the tropics. Desert house mice are sandy in color. City house mice are sooty. Mice from the Himalaya Mountains are extra dark.

Beatrix Potter, say the experts, did the house mouse's portrait perfectly in the books she wrote and illustrated for children. She caught the sharp snout, the big ears, the dark fur and the tail as long as head and body together. No one would confuse her Johnny Town Mouse with her field mice, which are short tailed and white about the underparts.

75

For current studies, in order to tell one house-mouse species from the six others, scientists do all sorts of chromosome counts and gene banding. They are choosy about the quality of specimens, saying that only ten percent in the drawers are of any use to them for these tests.

The trouble is that many of the mice have simply been caught by mistake when people were looking for something else, probably something bigger or more exotic. (One botanist sent in, from the

House mouse specimens are cotton-filled skins, the skulls saved separately in bottles.

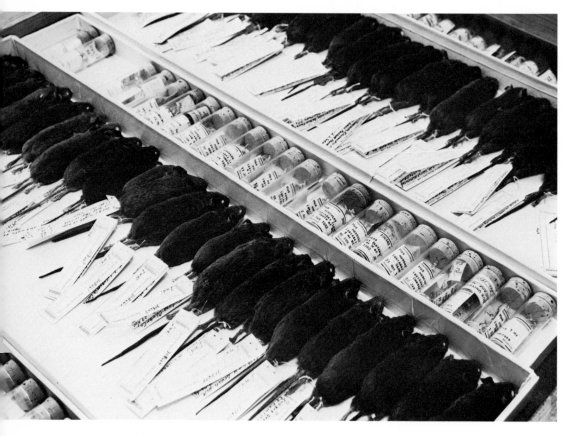

field, mice caught by his cat while the man was digging desert plants. Birdwatchers send skeletons they find in pellets regurgitated by owls.) Many of the mouse skulls have been cracked by digging tools or rattled to bits in sieves or broken by snap traps. Delicate bones have been poked out of line with forceps or dislocated in boiling. Mice for specimens, it seems, should never be boiled.

To prepare a mouse, mouse experts say, first measure its total body length and its tail and its ear and one hind foot, then skin the animal, dry it, and feed it to dermestid beetles in a box. The dermestids will clean it quickly, overnight. Without damaging or disarranging the pieces, they will eat away the meat and leave a perfect skeleton.

One mouse that recently arrived at the museum through the mail was accompanied by a letter. The donor had seen the animal scampering about in a warehouse at an Antarctic research station. "Can this be a house mouse?" he wrote.

"It can be. It is," was the answer. "And thank you for our first Antarctic house mouse."

The gift mouse is the same *Mus domesticus* that was in on the beginnings of Western civilization. It's the same species a mouse expert catches today inside his museum desk when he has tucked a bag of cookies in a drawer and forgotten them.

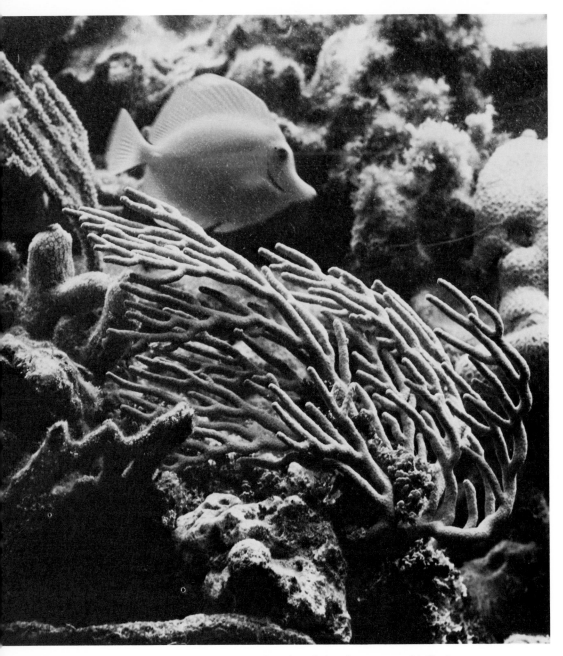

Live gorgonian in the coral-reef tank bends as waves buffet it.

Gorgonian

THE gorgonian lives in a glowing tank with fish darting all about. It looks like a bush, bending with the waves' buffeting and bobbing up again, anchored by its holdfast. It's a coral, an animal, with mouthparts all along its "branches." Without the waves to scour it and to scatter out bits of food, it would be dead in a day.

The wave makers are a pair of buckets above the tank at the deep end, side by side. One bucket holds eight gallons; the other, five. So they tip at different rates as they fill with water, sending out waves large and small. Once every minute when both buckets spill together, there's a sparkling crash that sets the fish racing and the gorgonian rocking hard. At the shallow end, a wave catcher keeps the waves from bouncing back in an endless washing-machine slish and slosh.

Watching over the waves and all the reef-tank equipment is a 365-days-a-year job, Christmas included. Water must be tested twice a day for how hot it is, how acidic, how salty, and the lamps must be checked to be sure the simulated sunrise is at six in the morning. A bank of switches turns on the lamps in sequence for a scorching long day and a synchronized dusk. Night falls at 10 P.M.

The tank's glass needs a squeegee wipe every 48 hours. And each week algae must be harvested from the screens on which they

The coral reef exists like an oasis in the midst of this marine desert. The highest rates of primary productivity measured anywhere on earth occur in water from the ocean flowing over the reef. To find out why, scientists travel to reefs to conduct experiments. As a result of these experiments, scientists have been able to create in the laboratory this living reef, which serves as a tool for further

Coral-reef technician checks that a holdfast holds fast.

grow, up above the tank out of sight. In the ocean there would be miles and miles to a reef. Here water from the tank circulates up onto the screens, which give extra surfaces for algae to grow on. The algae form great, green mats, using up animal waste and giving off oxygen. In the process they cleanse the tank and keep down its fuzz.

Sea water lost by evaporation is replaced automatically by distilled water. No chemicals are added to the tank and scarcely any food—only two teaspoons a day of shrimp, one quarter cup of brine shrimp, and two goldfish for the barracuda.

Once a month chief reef technician Jill Johnson enters the tank.

She moves aside the lamps and climbs in at the deep end for an hour's maintenance. Sometimes she does it during the day with people watching. Mostly though she works at night. She wears a mask with a mouthpiece attached by a garden hose to a scuba tank in the lab. She wears weights, shorts, black stockings and often a wet-suit top. The stockings are to discourage damsel fish, who, she's discovered, are very territorial. They attack her legs with sharp nips.

If a coral has been knocked over by a fish or an urchin, she straightens it. If the gorgonian is looking riddled with snail holes, she moves the snail. The gorgonian is up front where it gets a lot of attention from the public because it's a daytime feeder. People standing close to the glass can see the polyps inside the tubes, filtering food. They get a better idea of the coral-as-animal from the gorgonian than they do from the brain coral, which looks just like a rock till it puffs out impressively in the dark.

A co-worker standing in front of the tank guides the technician as she adds new corals, telling her to shift one a tad to the left or the right. New corals arrive from the Caribbean in picnic coolers with bubbler attachments. In just ten hours from when they were washed by real waves they are washed by waves from buckets. Gorgonians get placed, as they live in the sea, halfway between the shallows and the deep.

The tankful that Jill Johnson tends is a first anywhere, not just a supersize fishbowl but a whole ecosystem, a reef in a box. Her community of 300 animals and plants (including 68 kinds of algae) is still not as complex as a real reef. All the same it is tricky work to keep it in balance. There was one near-disaster when the algae bloomed, the water turned to pea soup, and it took days to filter it clean again. Then there was the day a pump broke and spilled out 100 gallons of water. That was a day for mops.

Skull of 72-foot blue whale has suffered grievous accidents.

Whale Skull

THE whale skull hangs neatly in the air like a stripped-down white speedboat. Getting it here was a job involving whale-size quandaries and mishaps.

When the whale was caught on a June day in 1903 off the coast of Newfoundland, a man from the museum waited for it on the dock with measuring tapes in his pocket. He was wishing it to be even bigger than it was, for although a 72-foot–6-inch blue whale is impressive, he had his heart set on a 75-footer. He intended to stun people with the skull at the St. Louis world's fair and then to bring it back to the museum.

He agonized over his choice. Should he take this blubbery colossus quickly, while he had the chance, before it was whacked up and hauled to the cookers for its oil? Or should he hold out a bit longer, hoping for one that was bigger?

The men off the whaling ships couldn't help him. They'd landed bigger whales in the weeks before. Where had he been? They might land a bigger one again. They might not. They might not even match what he had. The season for whale hunting was past its peak.

From the whaling station, Fred Lucas (the same man who dug great auk bones) wrote troubled letters to his boss back in Washington. He was measuring whales from each day's catch. He was hacking his way into them, which he had to do to check if the skulls

These days, with a ban on whale killing, a museum gets its whales from strandings. With word that a dead whale has washed up on a beach, a team heads out by truck with foul-weather slickers and boots, with buckets, jars and big flensing knives like sharp-edged hockey sticks. The men and women mostly do their measurements and autopsy right on the beach. They save out the reproductive tract as evidence of maturity and the parasites and pieces of scar tissue as evidence of attackers (silver-dollar-size scars from the cookie-cutter shark; bigger scars, jagged and irregular, from bull shark teeth; and still others from the sucker discs of squid tentacles). They bottle the stomach contents to pick through later in the lab in order to remove the fish earbones. These tough little bones tell them which kinds of fish, how big and how many this whale ate in the last days of its life.

As for the whale itself, the practice until recently was to haul the carcass off the beach into any handy scrub where it could rot away for some months and then be put through a car wash. Now, though, the museum has a grand new whale-rendering plant, big as a gym, with a giant cookpot for boiling off the blubber. One wall clanks open, and chain hoists lift the body. A messy process is simpler but it is still messy. The men still wade through gore and grease, which doesn't seem to faze such scholars of whale biology.

were deformed or damaged. Now deep in gore and grease, he was causing traffic jams on the dock. And with each day's work he grew greasier.

In the end he stuck with what he had, and he was glad. For the skull measured 19 feet, 4 inches, only 2 inches short of a 75-footer's skull. Not bad, he thought. But he had not anticipated all

They even seem to like it, though they say that fellow passengers on the bus going home from work give them funny looks for the smell.

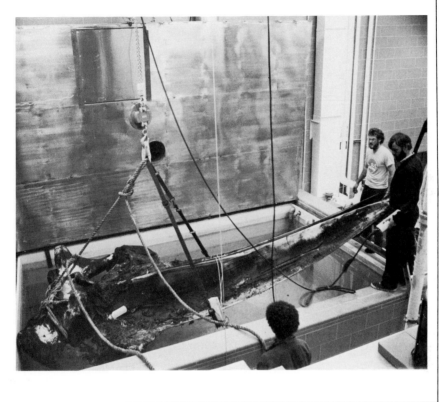

the difficulties of handling it. Just raising the nose, or trying to, he broke a huge timber he was using for a lever. Even with chain hoists and winches it took hours for a crew to flip the skull over.

To pack all three tons of it for shipping was, he wrote, a "puzzling" undertaking. He left some meat on the skull to protect it, and he built a crate that weighed four tons. The crate was big as

Rigger hoisting the whale skull learned his knots in Boy Scouts.

a room, braced like a railroad bridge, and fit inside a boxcar with just six inches left over. Proud Lucas, his letters sounding cheerier, called his crate a "corker."

That was 80 years ago, and accidents have occurred since then. In a warehouse where the skull was stored, a forklift truck crashed into it and greatly damaged it. Then, only ten years ago, the two whale specialists entrusted with its care, James Mead and Charles Potter, damaged the skull further—on purpose. They say it was either that or rip out the front of the Natural History building to enlarge the doors. They look sheepish telling how it happened, but they broke up the skull, or what was left of it, into three major pieces. They lit into it and banged away and yanked, all to get it into the museum for exhibit.

86

Then, when they had all the parts on the floor—by this time more than 100—a man from the vertebrate paleontology preparation lab (who happened to be fresh out of dinosaur work) was asked to put the skull back together right where it lay and to make it strong enough to hang from the ceiling. John Ott, who got the job, was discouraged at the start. He'd walk around the rubble on the floor, picking up a broken chunk or two from the pile and putting it down again. One of the chunks was as big as a canoe and not very strong either. Grease left in the bone had weakened all of it. But then with just a minimum of grumbling, which everyone thought he was entitled to, Ott set to work.

He cleaned away layers of grime and did the three-dimensional patchwork. Then he drilled holes into the bone to hold steel rods covered with pipes. And he attached cables to the pipes for lifting.

Now the skull, which has had more adventures than most, seems to float. People aren't aware of Ott's work. But for someone standing on the balcony and looking at the skull head-on, the main pipe is plain to see. It's like looking down the barrel of a rifle.

Storing whale skulls, let alone hanging them, is a giant headache. In the past they've been stashed in odd, hard-to-reach spaces: under the museum's outdoor flights of stairs and in hangars crammed with old airplanes. Now each one has its own cradle,— a kind of boat trailer on wheels, custom-built. A student of whales can look from skull to skull and compare a finback skull with a humpback or a right, a minke, a gray or a sperm whale skull as he pleases. In new quarters, the 30 skulls are in a line like a fleet of great upended yachts.

Terror, a substitute performer at the Insect Zoo, is a live tarantula with a dependable appetite.

Tarantula

TERROR, big as a fist, is a Mexican orange-kneed tarantula with a fur-ball body and eight jointed legs that stick out all around. She is black and hairy and has orange knees that are hairy too. Terror lives at the Insect Zoo next to the hall of bones. And she's a performer. Of course, *all* the creatures at the zoo perform. They're alive and creeping, jumping, munching. But Terror goes on show by appointment.

"Tarantula Feedings," the sign says, "daily at 10:30, 11:30 and 1:30." Terror's blood-and-guts act is a big crowd attracter. People flock to a tarantula anyway, even between feedings. They advance on its cage and retreat and clutch at their throats and come back again to look closer. Because a tarantula is a big daytime sleeper, one person asks and then another, "Is it dead?" Then when it rouses up and walks about they call it gross.

On a Thursday at 1:30 Henry Gemmill is the feeder. A white-coated Insect Zoo volunteer, he hollers out across the room that the feeding will begin. He's holding the cage, a clear plastic box. And once he mentions that tarantulas can jump six feet, people pull back into a wide circle.

Henry (which is how he introduces himself) then sits cross-legged, the cage on the carpet beside him, its lid removed for good viewing. Some members of the crowd sit too. Others say they'll stand, to be ready for a fast exit as needed.

Since Terror is making no moves to escape, no moves at all, her keeper slips in a few words to clear her record. Though she's in the Insect Zoo, she's not an insect. Where insects have six legs and three body parts, she's an arachnid, like a tick, a spider, a scorpion, with eight legs and two body parts.

Her sting won't kill, and it won't make people dance till they drop, which is Hollywood scare talk. A tarantula sting hurts, but no worse than a bee sting.

All the same Henry will not be picking up Terror. Only members of the Tarantula Club are permitted to do that. They take a quiz and pass a test and then they may lift a tarantula, very gingerly, placing their fingers on its sides between the second and third sets of legs.

Henry is not a member and he doesn't even want to be. The rule for people like him is that *if* his tarantula escapes he must put it back by lifting it on the cage lid. It's safer that way for his fingers and safer for Terror, who, if she's upset, may shoot out stinging hairs from her abdomen and get kind of bald looking.

In the wild, Henry says, such an orange-kneed tarantula as Terror would live in a burrow or hole in the ground in the desert, and its web wouldn't be to catch anything but to make the place comfortable. Here at the Insect Zoo—Henry points to double doors marked "No Admittance"—Terror lives in the rearing room in a kind of apartment block of tarantula cages, where feeding times and names identify the occupants: "Sunday 1:30 Agatha" and "Wednesday 1:30 Michael Jackson." There used to be a Houdini, the Great Escape Artist, who'd climb fast to the ceiling the instant his cage was opened. But Houdini died of old age. Old for a male is 10 years, though Terror can live to be 20. "Lucky females!" says Henry.

Terror today is taking the place of Bitsy, who is off her feed and has been for months. Terror is not one of the 21 regulars, but since she always seems to have an appetite, she's a reliable backup.

At this point Henry holds up what looks like a dead tarantula. It's Terror's old outgrown skeleton, whole but empty. He hands around bits of a broken one to touch—for the velvety feel of it. He tells how climbing out is a tricky and exhausting business, how she strains and pumps herself up and emerges wet as a newborn chick. It takes 24 hours to do and another 24 for her to harden up again. "It's almost awful to watch. You wish you could help."

Henry warns today's watchers against disappointment. He has a cricket ready in a bottle. It's the only food Terror gets all week—no snacks between meals. But Terror may not be hungry. Tarantulas are cold-blooded and don't move around much. They are not big eaters. They need water, but they can live for two years without eating if they have to.

Mostly, Henry says, they wait for a meal to meander close. As he speaks, he drops the cricket into the cage. It hops about on the sand. Terror appears not to notice. She has eight eyes, says Henry, but her sight is miserable. She won't know the cricket is there till it blunders into her or till her hairs pick up the vibrations. Even then, if she's not hungry, she won't kill it.

"She's hungry," says Henry. Anyone in the crowd who blinked an eye has missed Terror's pounce. Henry tilts up the cage for everyone to see. Terror's long fangs are stuck into the insect and she is pumping in the digestive juice that paralyses and kills it, turning its insides to liquid. She'll keep at the meal for half an hour and more, sucking, and she'll discard the husk at the end as if it were the carton from a milk shake.

The crowd begins to scatter. The lid is fastened to the cage with a screwdriver, and Volunteer Henry is off to other duties. He has hatchlings to see to in the rearing room and tobacco plants and roses to tend. Their leaves, never sprayed with insecticides, are a year-round source of insect lunches. He has other Insect Zoo creatures

Insect Zoo volunteers did the gluing of a cockroach mob caught in the act of scrabbling. The point of the exhibit is that Nature produces in abundance. If the offspring of one roach pair survive for three generations, then a kitchen like this one becomes a disaster area, and the cook copes with 130,000 roaches.

The dead roaches for the glue job came as a gift from the U.S. Department of Agriculture. At the museum they were freeze-dried to keep them from rotting, and then they were sprayed with insecticide. Not, it seems, with enough. For before the gluers began their work, tiny dermestid beetles had invaded the buckets of roaches and done quite a bit of chewing.

It was lucky the damage happened here to these all-alike members of the most common household species, *Blattella germanica,* which are nothing more than props for show. If there'd been nibbling at any of the 117,000 roaches in the study collection upstairs (where each roach is labeled with when it was collected, by whom and where), there'd have been an awful commotion.

As it was, work went ahead. It was slow and meticulous. Some high-school student volunteers carried kitchen panels home and bags of bugs to glue at odd moments. They'd spell out "Hi, Mom!" and "Tina" and draw a giraffe in bug bodies and then camouflage their jokes with more roaches. Now visitors photograph each other in front of the roach kitchen. No one has complained that the total number is not 130,000. Work stopped 50,000 short.

to feed too, with fruit and flowers and puppy kibbles, and still others to hand around as people ask, please, to hold a tobacco hornworm or a Madagascar hissing cockroach.

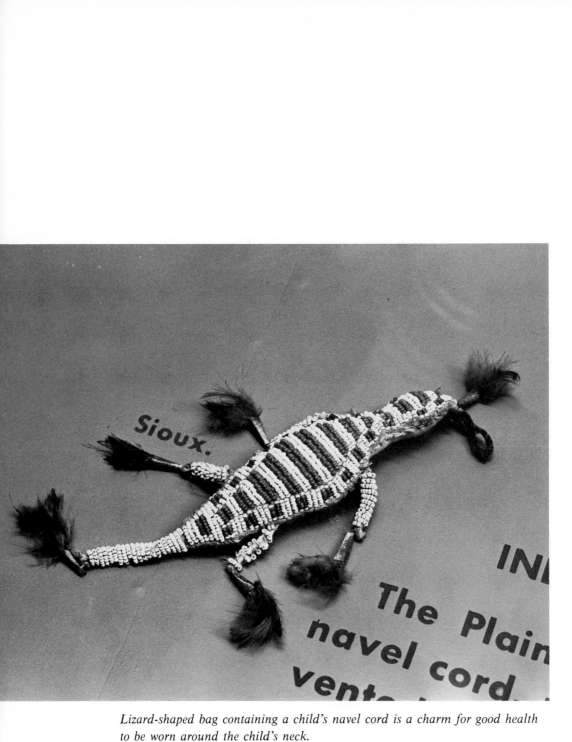

Lizard-shaped bag containing a child's navel cord is a charm for good health to be worn around the child's neck.

Navel-Cord Bags

TWO on exhibit are shaped like turtles, one (pictured here) like a lizard, one like a horned toad. At the birth of a Plains Indian baby, the navel cord was saved. It was dried and placed in a little bag such as these. A mother or a grandmother stitched the bag and decorated it and gave it to the child to wear about the neck as a charm against illness. When anthropologist John Ewers looks at these charms through the glass, he sees in his mind's eye a fifth one that isn't here, to his mind the prettiest of all. It isn't here for a good reason.

Ewers saw it just once, in the hands of the oldest-looking woman he'd ever met. He was living then, in the 1940s, on the Blackfeet Indian Reservation where he'd lived for several years. And he was seeking out the oldest people there, the "bow and arrow Indians," to hear from them about long-ago times: how they trained their horses and equipped them and hobbled them and picketed them and treated them for short breath or sore feet and got them to go with commands of "sh sh sh sh" and to stop or be silent with "ka ka ka ka." Weasel Tail would tell about riding out on buffalo hunts and how his wife, before she had children, came with him on raids, not to cook or do camp chores, but to capture enemy horses with the rest. And short, slight Elk-Hollering-in-the-Water would tell of her raiding, too. So it was not surprising for a boy to rush

95

into Ewers's office one late afternoon and urge him to come see his grandmother. And of course Ewers welcomed the chance.

It was the time of the sun dance, a tribal religious ceremony, and many Indians were gathered nearby. The boy said the grandmother had something to show, to sell maybe for a museum.

I followed him to the entrance of one of the tipis in the camp circle and he invited me in. Within the dimly lighted lodge I became aware of a single person sitting on a blanket to my left. She was a bent-over, deeply wrinkled woman who looked older than any other Indian I ever had met. The teen-ager introduced me to his grandmother, and then rather gruffly, I thought, asked her to show me the article that he believed I might purchase. Slowly she withdrew a small packet from the bosom of her dress. Her frail hand quivered as she held it out for me to examine. It proved to be the most handsomely beaded navel cord amulet that I had ever seen.

She told me this packet contained her own navel cord; that it had always been carried close to her body; and that I could see it had ensured her a very long life. She had thought it ought to be buried with her, but her grandson was suggesting that it might be sold to the museum.

As the grandson pressed me to make the old lady an offer, her eyes filled with tears. She reached out her hand for the amulet and gathered it in both arms to her breast. Clearly that lady needed that amulet much more than did the museum. I thanked her as graciously as I could for permitting me to see her beautiful treasure—and left the tipi.

When the Indians hall was rebuilt 20 years back, Ewers had to make the choices of what to show, what not to. He had to be tough

96

on himself not to overstuff the space. He chose one Plains pad saddle (the pillowy kind used for fast travel) and one woman's saddle (high in front, high in back) and a sturdy chicken-snare saddle that was used for transport. On his list he had 87 nonfood uses for the buffalo —from robes and parfleches (the Indians' suitcases) to berry bags and kickballs. He could never fit in an example of each one. A few he didn't even have, such as rawhide horseshoes and sleds with rib-bone runners.

Of course he put on show the one-of-a-kind Indian spectaculars, like the 1866 Winchester rifle of Sioux Chief Sitting Bull and the huge Arapaho tipi made of 14 buffalo-cow skins, which had been folded in the attic for 90 years. And he showed the common things *because* they were common. Moccasins were long the most popular collectible. They were cheap and useful as slippers. Soldiers bought them as souvenirs of service in Indian country. Ewers put in the moccasins and a simple digging stick as well. Every Plains Indian woman had one for digging wild turnips, yet such a stick is a rare sight in museums because who'd think to save or collect one?

Almost every Plains Indian had a navel-cord bag, too. Many were buried with their owners or burned when the owners converted to Christianity. Some were carried away by missionaries as evidence of "savagery." Ewers chose four to show, always remembering the fine one that was buried, he believes, with the old woman at her death.

Blue-eyed Egyptian bull mummy was x-rayed with the help of the navy.

Bull Mummy

THE bull mummy lies as it might in a field, watching. It has the shape still of an Egyptian bull. But its fancy paint job is gone, along with its crisp outline. Scraps have fallen off. The wrappings hang loose in flaps.

Conservators, from the conservation lab, take care of this ancient lumpy bundle. They see to it that the temperature in the glass case won't cook it, or humidity rot it, or creatures eat it for its glue.

They protect it, too, by not rushing in to spruce it up, by *not* bleaching it, *not* patching on the scraps, *not* regluing. Bleaches might damage the fibers; patches might go in the wrong places; glues might interfere with old glues and spoil a future look at the mummy materials.

All the same, without poking into it harmfully, these people needed to know about the body inside. Sacred bulls such as this one—and cats, birds, crocodiles—had been pampered in life. At death they'd been mummified, treated in the same way as human beings with ritual oils, salts and spices to preserve them. Their souls, which were believed to have fled at death, might then rejoin perfect bodies for an everlasting life.

After two thousand years, how *was* this body? Was it decomposing? Collapsing? Had it been wrapped with bones all in place, shin bone attached to knee bone? Or did the bones lie in bundles?

One man, laid out rigid, looks like a stone carving. He is not freeze-dried, not mummified. Wilhelm von Ellenbogen, according to the label, died and was buried in 1792 in Philadelphia. When groundwater seeped into his body, it turned him to a kind of hard soap, called adipocere. It preserved his features from head to toe, including his knee-length ribbed stockings.

The body, which surfaced in 1875 when roads were cut through a cemetery, came into the hands of a professor of anatomy. Later it was a gift to the museum, where textile experts, checking it out, said Mr. E's socks are silk and his underwear—that's as far as anyone probed—is cotton.

People also checked the name. No Ellenbogen appears in city directories for the 1790s or in lists of deaths either. It's known that the body turned up just when the professor was midway through his lecture on bones of the arm, making his yearly joke about the funny bone. It's guessed that *Ellenbogen,* as the German word for elbow, came to mind as he wrote his label.

There's nothing bogus about the body. Such a turning to soap does happen. But once a year a telephone call comes to the museum—sometimes *for* a Mr. Ellenbogen, sometimes *from* him—on April Fools' Day.

One cat mummy on exhibit has its body—head to tail—inside. So have the hawk and the crocodile. The second cat has its bones in a bundle at the bottom.

To x-ray the bull, the naval lab offered the use of its equipment (big enough to x-ray boats). The pictures were a surprise. They show that the mummy contains not a bull but a jumble of trash. There is no body inside treated with ritual anything. There's a skull where

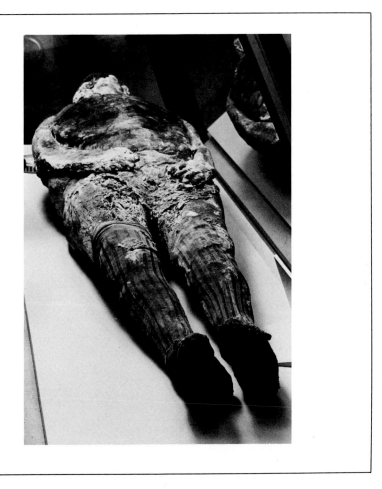

it belongs, with real horns, but the body is a wood frame filled with sticks and scraps, rags and bones. The bones come from several animals at that.

Was it a 200 B.C. rip-off? So it seems. Bull worship was changing. These mummy makers took shortcuts. Never mind mummifying such a huge body. It was a long process—tedious. Wild dogs often ran off with pieces and mixed them. A bull head, it may have

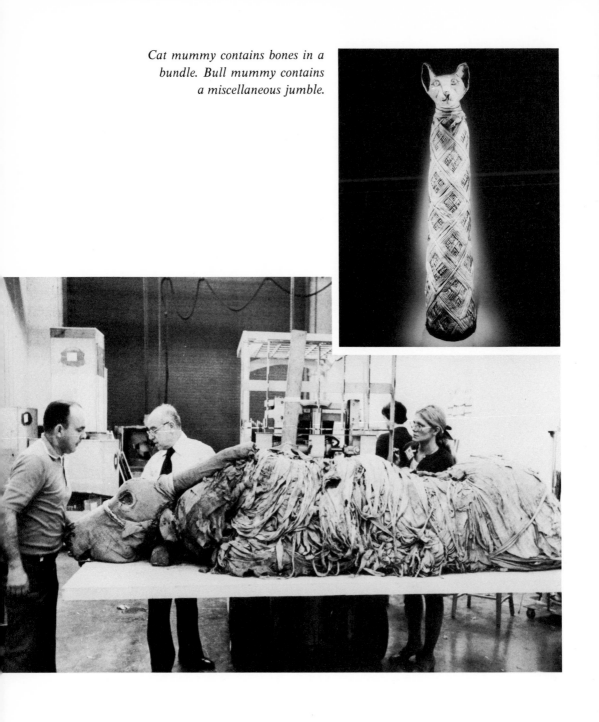

Cat mummy contains bones in a bundle. Bull mummy contains a miscellaneous jumble.

been thought, would do, along with a bull shape, wrapped and painted.

The painting on this bull was once fine, in blues, greens, gold. No one skimped on it or on the eyes either, which are beautifully formed of glass set in stone. Bright blue, they look out in a jaunty way, as if they know a secret.

Visitors to the Discovery Room can answer a naturalist's question (below) with the help of a photographic clue (right).

How did the hole get there?

Stumpers

A blocky rock is a stumper in the Discovery Room. Here all rocks are touchable, along with Indian dolls, weeds, furs, seeds and teeth. The stumpers are intended to stir people into looking closely at things and pondering. They are tagged with big question marks.

People lifting this rock run a hand over its hollow. They guess that water scooped it out, the way a torrent carved the Discovery Room's boulder. There's something kind of mechanical looking, though, about the squared edges, which makes people doubtful. If they give up and flip the tag over, they read—in print or in braille—that the block is made of compressed salt. It's a salt lick, a rock all right, but the hollow was sculpted by tongues.

The farmer at Juniper Ledge dairy farm in Massachusetts buys such a block each year from a seed and feed store (price $5). He puts it out in the pasture for his cows and for passing deer. It just occurred to him, because he'd enjoyed the Discovery Room on a visit, that this block of his had been worn away to a nice shape. He mailed it to the museum in a shoe box along with a photograph of Diana, his cow, rolling out her tongue for a lick.

Who wouldn't be stumped by bezoars—shiny, smooth balls, surprisingly light? The ones in the Naturalist Center, also a place

The larger of two hair balls has been cut in half to show felt-like matted hair inside.

for touching and guessing, range from golf ball size to baseball size. The largest one was brought in by a farmer from South Carolina. He'd found it lying on the ground in his pasture and was thoroughly puzzled. The first staff person who looked at it thought it might be a fossilized sponge. It looked like one but it seemed too light. The second person to look at it led the visitor to a drawer with bezoars like his—stony spheres that form inside cows or deer or buffalo or llamas.

The balls are formed of hair that has been licked and swallowed. In time and with much swirling about in stomach juices, they take on a hard covering like the shell of an egg. Most such hair balls aren't discovered till after the animal has died from other causes. How this one appeared on the ground is a mystery.

When it was cut open at the Center, the donor stepped back, expecting a stench. But the hair inside was clean, dry, and solidly matted, like felt, and it had no smell at all.

In the Middle Ages bezoars were prized. They were thought to be a remedy against disease. Some were made into goblets and handsomely fitted with jeweled stems.

One rock in the Naturalist Center has caused a lot of grief. For eight years it was thought to be a coprolite, a fossilized dropping, from a dinosaur. People picked it up with grins on their faces and bemused expressions. They came back with friends. And they asked about other such droppings. The museum doesn't have a lot of coprolites, only a few hundred, because out in the field they're usually not recognized for what they are.

Some in the study collections, the paleontologists brag, are as handsomely shaped as cake decorations. Some are also unusually valuable, especially the ones found along with Pleistocene-Age skeletons in a dry cave in Arizona. One large cabinet is filled with the great loaves from giant sloths, clumps from mountain sheep, and pellets from rabbits, none of which hardened to rock. "Add water," says one of the scientists, "and they're good as new!" These coprolites are much scrutinized for their clues to animal diet and digestion and for what the seeds and pollen in them tell of Pleistocene vegetation. Still other coprolites have bones or beaks or teeth inside them that yield further clues.

It just happened that one paleontologist taking a careful look

Lumpy rock (left) is not after all a coprolite (a fossilized dropping) though rocks at right are.

at the Naturalist Center's "coprolite" had his doubts. For so smooth a one, it had unlikely lumps in an unlikely arrangement. He carried it away for consultation. When he brought the specimen back, shaking his head from side to side to say No, it was not a coprolite, one visitor who was present said, "You are going to see a grown woman cry." The director of the Center said, "How do you think *we* feel—misleading people all these years?" The paleontologist said, "Misidentification. It happens often in science." And he brought a gift to the Naturalist Center as consolation.

Now the rocks lie in a drawer side by side. Two—the gift—are coprolites of the Lower-Permian (260-million-year-old) shark. They have a twist caused by the spiral valve in the shark's intestines. The other is a chunk of iron ore that *looks* like a coprolite.

Guard dog Max and his handler, a K-9 team, patrol the museum at night.

Max

MEET Max, a German shepherd with stand-up ears, a quick frisky step and a let's-get-going attitude. He's a protector of the great auk, *Antrodemus* and the rest—the dog half of a guard-dog team that patrols all the buildings of the Smithsonian Institution. There's a chance of seeing him in the late afternoons, for he comes on duty at four and works till midnight.

At home with the guard, Max is playful and silly, rolls on the floor with the four children, gives rides on his back, acts like the fifth kid in the family. On the job he sticks strictly to business. That doesn't mean he's mean. He's not. But Max on the job is serious.

A museum isn't a bank, and guarding it is different. Here people are expected to come by the big yellow bus loads. Yet the treasures they come to see are not to be snatched away or damaged. The bones and plants are a record of life. And no amount of money can buy replacements. A guard is caught in a kind of fix—to be open and generous but not to vandals. Max helps. He gives a wag-tail welcome. And if necessary he attacks.

Max was picked at the start for his good health and his good looks and because he has the right kind of aggressiveness. Museum canines—K-9s—have to be large. Max weighs 85 pounds. Their ears must stand up and their teeth must be perfect. A dog who's unfriendly to children never gets into the corps. A dog who's shy or gun-shy, and doesn't get over it, flunks out. Some flunk because they can't get used to marble floors. One of Max's classmates would go spread-eagle on the slick marble and lie quivering till he was carried off to the concrete or grass he was used to.

Max took well to the training, where rewards along the way were not treats or snacks but "Good boy!" "Good dog!" "Good Max!" and a lot of fur rumpling. His classes included jumping and ladder climbing and wall scaling, even drinking out of museum drinking fountains, and a series of lessons in Search! and Fetch! to find pocketbooks, wallets, loose cash and car keys in the shrubbery.

Max excelled in these and in finding hidden people—like ones who stay on inside after the museum's closing or who break in. He also mastered the standard course in lost children, of which there are many—one lost child an hour, two in the summertime. Outdoors on the mall, the K-9 teams are easy to spot. Lost people come to them and reunions take place quickly. Even inside in the maze of exhibits, no child is lost for more than five minutes.

After 14 weeks' training, Max had learned to lunge for a gun arm on command and to hold fast. And he'd learned to stop in his tracks on a command recall. Trainers say the hardest thing of all is to teach a dog to bite. Max learned.

Max was one of 8 dogs to graduate from a class of 40. Now he and his handler understand each other so well they read each other's signals. They almost read each other's minds. Max's ears going forward and a special stillness about him mean something's not quite right. A change in the guard's voice or his pace means, Watch it around the next corner!

On an ordinary Tuesday, Max and his handler patrol the grounds. They check the door locks (all okay) and the loading docks, where barrels of fish are hoisted in on their way to a lab. As the last visitors are leaving, the team enters by the front door to do the sweep of the building. Theirs is the kind of tour anybody else might envy. No jostling in crowds, no standing three deep to reach the coral reef. Just one dog and one man walking briskly with no other sounds but squeaky shoes and dog toenails on the marble and from time to time a bit of conversation.

Max walking the halls is lively and alert. It's the work he enjoys, not the exhibits. Nose down, tail up, he sniffs along the floor. Then, head up, he sniffs the drafts for what they carry. He's seeking what he's been trained to seek—the scent of people.

If *Diplodocus* was missing or *Antrodemus,* let alone the Hope diamond, Max wouldn't see the difference. But if someone was on top of a showcase or behind a dinosaur or a closed metal door, Max wouldn't be fooled for an instant. He'd pass the word fast to his handler. If the person didn't respond when asked, and if the command to the dog was "Find 'em!" Max would let out his Max howl—a kind of cry, kind of song—and start running. Whether or not he attacked would depend on the commands. (Max wasn't taught the howl in school. He invented it.)

Max's lack of interest in the exhibits shows what a pro he is. A new dog on his first night's sweep growls at the Ice-Age mannequins. He raises his hackles at Teddy Roosevelt's giraffe and keeps looking back at the reared-up polar bears. Are they gaining on him?

Max moves past without a flicker, as if bears were nothing to him, or tigers leaping, or a pterosaur diving from the ceiling. Never mind the low eerie lights and the lunging skeletons, the odd shapes and shadows. In the Insect Zoo crickets are chirping and katydids calling and tarantulas moving about. On the dinosaurs' balcony the live crocodiles are rustling through their rushes. Max sticks to his sniffing.

In an hour he's covered the exhibit halls and started on the space beyond—the offices and labs and attics. Here some of the sights may be unsettling for his handler: the rooms of jars filled with pickled things, the racks of skins, the freeze-dry lab where snakes hang from light fixtures. But the spooky look doesn't spook Max.

"It's old hat to Max," says his handler. So are the museum smells, which are sort of musty, sort of mothbally. And so are the comings and goings of people. Here in the work part of the museum he expects to see them: a husband and wife team pinning their beetles, a botanist floating seaweeds onto paper, others tracking blips on computer screens.

Some nights there are coffee pots to turn off or leaks to report. A night with smoke or a strange smell or a suspected break-in is a real workout.

On a balcony over the coral reef, eye level with the hanging whale model, one researcher tends her tanks of experiments. Her backpack and bike are propped by the desk for the trip home. As guard and dog approach in the dark she's peering into the brightly lit water. "The brain corals are awake and feeding," she says, "all puffed up like sofa cushions." Guard watches with her. Dog waits.

It's close to midnight, close to time for this team to sign out. Tip has come on duty, and his bark is heard out in the rotunda. As Max begins his trit-trot back down the ramp, the reef researcher calls after him, "Thanks for looking in, Max."

Baird's sandpiper.

WHETHER you dash through the museum or dawdle, give a thankful thought to Spencer Fullerton Baird. There's no Founding Father Baird statue. There's no portrait of this man who described himself as a lanky "specimen of humanity, with red beard, rough hair, crooked legs and the biggest feet in Washington . . . eyes pea-green." Baird's friends said he was big in stature, in sympathies, in interests, that he was the most energetic and gentlest of men and that he looked and walked more like a farmer than like the nation's most eminent biologist.

You'll find Baird's name in two places. You'll find it in large letters on the doors to the museum's lecture hall: BAIRD AUDITORIUM (though Baird never gave a lecture if he could help it and never attended lectures because they put him to sleep). You'll find his name, too, about knee high, written small on the label of Baird's sandpiper.

People working at Natural History say the collections are Baird's monument. They say they feel a kinship with him for his glee in all the earth's "rich treasures." Perhaps you'll feel it, too, as you roam the halls of his museum.

Index

Numbers in *italics* indicate photographs.

L

508.074   Thomson, Peggy
Thom   Auks, rocks and the
           odd dinosaur : inside
           stories from the Smith-
           sonian's Museum of
           Natural History.

'90

DEMCO